BOREDOM,
SELF,
AND CULTURE

BOREDOM, SELF, AND CULTURE

Seán Desmond Healy

RUTHERFORD • MADISON • TEANECK
FAIRLEIGH DICKINSON UNIVERSITY PRESS
LONDON AND TORONTO: ASSOCIATED UNIVERSITY PRESSES

© 1984 by Associated University Presses, Inc.

Associated University Presses
440 Forsgate Drive
Cranbury, NJ 08512

Associated University Presses
25 Sicilian Avenue
London WC1A 2QH, England

Associated University Presses
2133 Royal Windsor Drive
Unit 1
Mississauga, Ontario
Canada L5J 1K5

Library of Congress Cataloging in Publication Data

Healy, Seán Desmond, 1927–
 Boredom, self, and culture.

 Bibliography: p.
 Includes index.
 1. Boredom. 2. Boredom—Social aspects. 3. Educational
psychology. 4. Meaning (Psychology) I. Title.
BF575.B67H42 1984   152.4   82-48607
ISBN 0-8386-3146-0

Printed in the United States of America

To my wife,
without whose constant
intellectual stimulation
and loving support
this book would
never have been written

Lord, take pity on the Christian who
doubts, on the unbeliever who
would fain believe, on the galley-slave
of life who puts to sea alone, in the
night, beneath a firmament no longer
lit by the consoling beacon-fires of the
ancient hope.

J. K. Huysmans

Contents

Preface

There is a strange haziness about the state commonly referred to as boredom. While the literature on it is quite limited, it nonetheless *has* one (most of it recent), unlike other states of mind such as joy, envy, or fear, and a literature moreover much of which is concerned not simply to describe its origins, operations, and effects, but to determine just what it actually *is*. What emerges is the rather puzzling fact that, again unlike other mental states, boredom has a complex and enigmatic past, and an ambiguous present. While it is generally paid scant and superficial attention, passed over lightly as transitory and insignificant, the ready made phrases of the language seem to tell a different tale: "bored to tears," "bored stiff," "bored silly," "bored to death," and, more recently, "bored out of one's skull."

Encountering boredom in the first few years of my career, in one of its most fertile breeding grounds, the school—or, more exactly, the classroom—these complexities were not as yet in the least apparent to me. The very institution in which the encounter took place, and outlook of those with whom I worked, whether students or teachers, served to suppress questions, for all tended to take what one might call the "trivial" view of boredom. This is the supposedly commonsense perception of it as a virtually unavoidable occupational hazard, disagreeable but harmless, possessed even it might be of redeeming educational value inasmuch as it prepares its victims for the greater boredom to come—a kind of educational vaccine stimulating the production of characterological antibodies to contain future onslaughts. Possessed of a low boredom-threshold, I soon found myself doing all I could, short of sacrificing education to entertainment or diversion, to holding the spectre at bay. I was at that stage as yet unaware even of boredom as potentially and incrementally corrosive and destructive, a major element in the genesis of the drop-out, the self-destroyer, the vandal, the violent, and the apathetic, much less of it as a silent scourge about whose cause there was any serious question or problem.

9

My early teacherly concern to keep boredom at bay stemmed far more from a quasi-instinctive dislike of boring my young charges (and myself into the bargain) than from any theoretically grounded understanding of, or objection to, it per se. It was only under Dr. Bruce Wilshire's tutelage at Rutgers University that I began to sense something of profounder significance hidden by the very banality of the common term—a classic instance of, to paraphrase Nietzche, the familiar being rendered virtually invisible by its very familiarity.

It was not difficult to establish that there was one characteristic common to all instances of boredom, present and past, namely the loss of a sense of personal meaning, whether in relation to a particular experience or encounter, or to an entire life-situation. This loss might be occasioned by the withdrawal or absence of the meaningful, or by the imposition of the unmeaningful, and in the vast majority of instances the precise irritant could be identified, even if not immediately. It was the discovery that quite often even the victims themselves could not pin down the reason for their chronic and painful boredom that suggested that there was more in the affliction than met the eye. There was boredom, evidently, and then again there was *boredom,* the former a normal human (and maybe even general mammalian) reaction when the inborn, interest-driven movement outward into the world is somehow impeded or cannot find an appropriate object, the latter an aberration peculiar to mankind, arising from no certainly assignable cause.

For clarity's sake I decide to label the inexplicable and persisting form 'hyperboredom,' and leave 'boredom' to stand for the everyday variety. Hyperboredom, under a host of terms, had not of course escaped the notice of observers as far back as Roman times, and it was the subject of comment and analysis by thinkers as diverse as St. Gregory the Great, St. Thomas Aquinas, Pascal, Kierkegaard, Freud, and Heidegger. But the very diversity of proposed explanations diminished the credibility of all of them to be seen as *the* explanation, which each assumed itself to be. While any one of them seemed likely to be able to explain some cases of hyperboredom, none of them even addressed itself to one of its most obvious features, its immensely increased prevalence in the last several hundred years in the West. All were firmly individualistic and psychological in their approach, rather as if one were to attribute the rising number of deaths on the roads in the last half century to behavioral idiosyncrasies rather than to the larger num-

ber of faster cars on a greatly extended network of roads during that
period of time.

There seemed to be room for a study that would look beyond
these exclusively personalistic explanations and seek a general
cause for an affliction that had grown to pandemic proportions, and
this is that study. As it started out from a consideration of how to
keep "trivial" boredom out of the classroom, so it concludes with
some reflections on what the school can and should do to combat
the drastic effects of its radical relative, hyperboredom. The prog-
nosis is not cheerful, for the disorder that I set out to examine
supposing that it was, though troublesome, benign (in the medical
sense), seems on closer examination to be one symptom of an
advanced stage of an entire culture in irremediable disintegration.

BOREDOM,
SELF,
AND CULTURE

1 • The Emergence of a Mood

Boredom depends on the nothingness which pervades reality
                                        Sören Kierkegaard

L'Ennemi se déguise en Ennui
Et me dit: "A quoi bon, pauvre dupe?"

                                        Paul Verlaine

There would at first glance seem to be no good reason for supposing that boredom, any more than any other mental or spiritual
state, should have steadily and continuously increased in modern
times. In fact, one might have supposed exactly the opposite, given
the vastly more numerous diversions and entertainments that have
become available, the increase in time for play, and the expansion
of opportunities for finding and pursuing constructive interests.
And yet the records of man's thought and experience indicate
otherwise, showing quite unmistakably that, while joy, anger,
love, hate, and the rest have continued to delight or to plague him
on a more or less constant level, boredom has a history and has
gradually emerged from near obscurity to center stage. The
strangeness of its growing presence in the last three centuries is
intriguing, all the more so because it has been so little remarked
upon. What was once a rare state of mind, confined at least in the
common estimation of later times to an effete elite, has now become the common property of the bored horde.[1] Once this development is perceived, a number of questions press for answers:
Just what *is* 'boredom'? Is it one or many? Where does it come
from? How widespread is it? What accounts for its growth? And,
above all, what does it mean for the individual and his society?
Surely something important must have occurred in the structure of
our world to account for the extent and virulence of an affliction
that lacked even a distinctive term in the English language until
well into the last century. Some understanding of the nature and
significance of the occurrence may perhaps suggest what can and
must be done if its ravages are to be resisted.

15

It is true, of course, that 'boredom' is often used to refer to feelings that are superficial and fugitive, feelings so common and of so little effect that the state is thought to be too trivial and banal to warrant any sustained attention. This very fact may indeed explain why there has been so little recognition that boredom has far more profound and destructive forms: they have been concealed, or rendered invisible, by the apparently inoffensive, even childish, aura that has surrounded the word. This has provided a semantic smokescreen behind which has lurked, and continues to lurk, a grave sickness of the spirit, potentially destructive of the individual and possibly even of society as a whole.[2]

There are isolated references to boredom in classical times, but the earliest detailed treatments of the emotional incubus are those recorded in the fourth-century accounts of the hermits of Lower Egypt—the Desert Fathers—which detail their encounters with the *daemon meridianus* ("noonday devil"), visitations that could devastate them, utterly sapping their energies in the pursuit of God, reducing them to blank lassitude, indolence, and despair. Cassian of Marseilles, writing in the fourth century, gives a detailed description that is so penetrating that it is worth quoting in extenso:

> Our sixth contending is with that which the Greeks call 'ακεδία[3] and which we may describe as tedium or perturbation of heart. It is akin to dejection [*tristitia*], and especially felt by wandering monks and solitaries, a persistent and obnoxious enemy . . . disturbing the monks especially about midday. . . .
>
> When this besieges the unhappy mind, it begets aversion from the place, boredom with one's cell and towards any work that may be done within the enclosure of our own lair, we become listless and inert. It will not suffer us to stay in our cell, or to attend to our reading . . . Towards eleven o'clock or midday, it induces such lassitude of body and craving for food as one might feel after . . . hard toil. Finally one gazes anxiously here and there, and sighs that no brother of any description is to be seen approaching: one is for ever in and out of one's cell, gazing at the sun as though it were tarrying to its setting: one's mind is in an irrational confusion . . . one is slothful and vacant in every spiritual activity, and no remedy, it seems, can be found for this state of siege than a visit from some brother, or the solace of sleep. Finally our malady suggests that in common courtesy one should salute the brethren, and visit the sick, near or far. It dictates such offices of duty and piety as to seek out this relative or that

. . . far better to bestow one's pious labour upon these than sit
without benefit, or profit in one's cell.[4]

The tormented hermits were suffering from the capital vice, the
vitium capitalis—so called because it was the *caput* ("head") from
which flowed many forms of sin—known to medieval man as *accidia*, or 'acedia'. Something, or everything, about their situation
sapped their spiritual energies; they could say with the psalmist,
"My soul slumbers on account of acedia," "slumbers" in the Gnostic
sense of losing any sense of their spiritual goal.[5] They were overtaken by a spiritual indifference or disgust, by a boredom with
their way of life so profound as to nauseate them. Under its onslaughts a monk's very being came to seem to him pointless in an
existence from which God had withdrawn. With the development
of Christianity into a religion of the people at large, the vice went
through immense complexities of definition and attribution as it
changed from being an exclusively eremitic affliction, an occupational hazard as it were, into a weakness capable of besetting any
Christian. Two elements, however, remained constantly associated
with it: physical laziness and sloth in regard to the performance of
religious duties *(otiositas)*, and spiritual indifference or boredom
with religious exercises and a loss of enthusiasm for the *opus Dei.*[6]
The spiritual aspect of *accidia* was profoundly and exhaustively
examined by Saint Thomas Aquinas, who saw the essence of the sin
as *tristitia de spirituali bono*, man's complete lack of interest in,
and rejection of, his spiritual good, which, since that is God himself, entails a radical rejection of being itself, one's own and everything else's. However, by the fourteenth century, 'slewthe' (sloth),
as the vice came to be called in Chaucer's English, was already
generally regarded as mainly if not exclusively a matter of laziness,
first in the service of God, and then gradually in the carrying out of
secular responsibilities.

The most exact anatomy of the vice in late medieval times was
made by Chaucer in "The Parson's Tale":

Accidie maketh hym hevy, thoghtful, and wraw [peevish, petu-
lant] . . . He doeth alle thyng with anoy, and with wrawnesse,
slacknesse, and excusacioun, and with ydelnesse, and un-
lust. . . . He loveth no bisynesse at al. It forsleweth and forslug-
geth . . . and they ne may neether wel do ne wel thynke. Accidie
comth first, that a man is anoyed and encombred for to dooth any
goodnesse . . . drede to bigynneth to werke any goode werkes.

He rekketh of no thyng. . . . Thanne comth the synne of worldly sorwe, swich as is cleped tristicia . . . Therof comth that a man is anoyed of his owne lyf. For certes, ther bihoveth greet corage agains Accidie, lest that it ne swolwe the soule by the synne of sorwe, or destroy it by wanhope.[7]

The word 'anoy' calls for comment, as it was from this Middle English version of the Late Latin *inodiare* ("to hold in hatred") that the French word for boredom, *ennui*, was formed sometime in the thirteenth century, and this notion of hatred—of one's life, of one's self—associated with the sin gives some vital clues to the nature of a type of boredom far deeper than mere passing tedium or monotony. Acedia, in the spiritual sense of *tristitia*, remained, however, the scourge of the religious and the scholarly life, of those who were relieved of some if not all of the day-to-day demands of survival and whose métier was contemplation and reflection. One may presume that those on whom life's necessities pressed almost incessantly, whose eyes were never far removed from the soil and whose minds were trameled by the narrow bounds of their existence, lacked either the leisure or the mental detachment from their immediate surroundings that are the sine qua non of this radical form of boredom.

But as early as the fourteenth century, in the brilliant culture of northern Italy, acedia came to assume in the work of Boccaccio, and even more in that of Petrarch, a secular form, an apparently entirely worldly one, though not apparently caused by the world. "The evil," Petrarch wrote, "has absolutely no apparent cause . . . it is like a voluptuousness in suffering that makes the mind sad," and it entails, "hatred and contempt of the human condition."[8] This bitter satisfaction in suffering marks a psychic shift toward what was later to be called 'melancholy'. During the later medieval period, as has been well said, "'acedia', 'tristitia', and 'melancholia', mixed and interpenetrated."[9] In the increasingly humanistic culture of late medieval and early modern Europe, however, the word 'accidie' disappeared from the English language, so that by the time Robert Burton came to write his exhaustive work on melancholy (first published in 1621), the word seems either no longer to have been available to him, in the sense of not being current, or at least no longer appropriate for some reason. The result is that he had to resort to Latin to describe the state of mind. *"Taedium vitae,"* he writes, is a common symptom, *tarda fluunt ingrataque tempora* time passes slowly and without enjoyment, they are soon tired of all things; they will now tarry, now be gone; now in bed they will rise, now up, then go to bed, now pleased, then again displeased; now they like, by and by dislike all, weary of all, *sequiture nunc vivendi nunc moriendo cupido* at one time they want to live, at another die . . . but most part *vitam damnant* they declare life not worth living, discontent, disquieted . . . often tempted, I say, to make away with themselves: *Vivere nolunt, mori nesciunt:* they cannot die, they will not live . . . they are weary of their lives, weary of all.[10]

This is the lone reference to *taedium vitae,* or to any state analogous to it (a state, that is, of apparently *inexplicable* boredom, of irrational and unaccountable disgust with life in toto) in *The Anatomy of Melancholy*—a fact that, taken in conjunction with its appearance only after several hundred pages in Burton's exhaustive work, rather suggests that it remained an unusual malady, still regarded as largely a theological concern, confined in its secular form to a mere handful of intellectuals. There was clearly some overlap between the symptoms of those who experienced—or who affected to experience—melancholy and those who were assailed by *accidia,* but this was a state that, for some uncertain reason, came to lack a distinctive name, in English at least. Cotgraves's *A Dictionarie of the French and English Tongues,* published in the first decade of the seventeenth century, in translating *ennui* (which had been employed in French as a synonym for 'acedia' since the thirteenth century),[11] lists only:

annoy; vexation; trouble; disquiet; molestation; sorrow; grief; anguish; wearisomeness; tediousnesse; irksomenesse; importunity; a loathing, or sacietie, of; a discontentment, or offence, at.[12]

'Wearisomenesse" brings to mind Burton's "weary of all," and Shakespeare himself had to use 'weary' for all degrees of boredom. In most, if not all, of its occurrences in his works—some twenty or so—it is clearly being used as an expression for normal boredom. "I stay too long by thee," says King Henry IV, "I weary thee," and nothing more is intended but that he has overstayed his welcome. Even in the case of Hamlet, boredom with existence as a whole would seem on the face of it to derive from a perfectly reasonable disillusionment with life in a young man whose father has been murdered with the connivance of a mother who has precipitately married—and incestuously at that, by the standard of the times—the assassin. Well might anyone in this situation declare with the prince,

> How weary, flat, stale, and unprofitable
> Seem to me all the uses of this world.

And yet, under the explicable ennui and the modish melancholy, there seems to lurk a supererogatory disgust for which there was no name. The English Malady, as melancholy came to be known, had somewhat the same sort of relationship to the "nameless woe" as did popular 'existentialism' to the thinking of Jean-Paul Sartre in more recent times—the causes might ultimately be the same, but the one was no more than a distant, feeble, and confused reflection of the image clearly seen by the other.

John Donne, who coined his own word, 'lethargies', for acedia, made much use of the word 'spleen' in a letter he wrote in 1622 referring to the prevalence of 'melancholy'.

> Every distemper of the body now, is complicated with the spleen, and when we were young men we scarce ever heard of the spleen. In our declinations now, every accident is accompanied with heavy clouds of melancholy; and in our youth we never admitted any. It is the spleen of the mind, and we are affected with vapours from thence.[13]

He is evidently no longer thinking about the condition that had earlier inspired him to write the despairing lines:

> What are we then? How little more alas
> Is man now, than before he was? he was
> Nothing; for us, we are nothing fit;
> Chance, or ourselves still disproportion it.
> We have no power, no will, no sense; I lye,
> I should not then thus feele this miserie.[14]

For the poet, 'lethargies' had been a phase, and he abandoned them and the poetry he had used to vent them when he became dean of Saint Paul's. His French contemporary, Pascal, was also able after years of struggle to transcend what he wrote of as "the state that defines man's structure."[15] Ennui, boredom, had become for him no longer *a* problem of man's existence, it had become *the* problem. The shift is a striking confirmation of what has been referred to as "the inner, deep-seated changes in the psyche during the early seventeenth century, the vital period for the emergence of modern European and American man." It is thus not so much that writers of the seventeenth century had "an ambivalent attitude toward ennui," as that there were in fact two coexisting conditions, one a normal and universal accompaniment of human living—however much inflated by posturing and rhetoric or by sociopolitical factors—the other deriving from an underlying cultural condition. The issue is confused by the fact that both of these had to be referred to indifferently in French as *'ennui'*, in English as 'melancholy' or a little later, 'spleen'. The clearest indication of this semantic problem occurs in one of La Rochefoucauld's *Maximes,* in which he writes that "l'extrême ennui sert à nous désennuyer." This is usually translated as "extreme ennui serves to distract us from boredom," but unless *ennui* means something different from the *ennui* at the root of *désennuyer,* it is difficult to see what the author is getting at. How could an extreme form of something distract one from a lesser form of the same affliction? The difficulty disappears with the realization that the words are being employed to refer to states or moods that are in essence already distinguishable but that are not yet distinctly denotable.

La Rochefoucauld was something of a connoisseur of boredom, complaining in his memoirs that he had spent "much time at the court in a state of boredom." As it happened, the establishment of the court at Versailles, within which the nobility were virtually sequestered in a society of institutionalized boredom, occurred at much the same time as the development of a radical personal boredom most penetratingly described by a sometime victim, Blaise Pascal. To him, man seemed driven on, inexorably, by "two secret contrary instincts." One drives him to seek excitement, the other, rest. Each betrays him, for

> we seek rest by struggling against certain obstacles and once they are overcome, rest proves intolerable because of the boredom it produces . . . We think either of present or of threatened miseries, and even if we felt quite safe on every side, boredom on its own account would not fail to emerge from the depths of our hearts, where it is naturally rooted, and poison our whole mind.
>
> Man is so unhappy that he would be bored even if he had no cause for boredom, by the very nature of his temperament, and

he is so vain that, though he had a thousand and one basic reasons for being bored, the slightest thing, like pushing a ball with a billiard cue, will be enough to divert him.[16]

For Pascal himself, the answer lay in an act of faith, or rather in a visitation of grace: "Happiness is neither outside us nor inside us; it is in God, both outside and inside us."[17] But as for the ranks of the nobility at Versailles, who continually complained of boredom, there is no reason to suppose that they were suffering from anything more profound than a lack of anything worthwhile to do.

Various forms of boredom flourished in contemporary England, lumped together with melancholy and depression under the term 'spleen', and by 1733 the latter was so common as to form the entire subject matter of a medical treatise published in that year entitled *The English Malady*. For the most part, its victims seem to have been oppressed by a generalized gloom, a "lowness of spirits," which, it was suggested, "may arise from the general uncertainty and many changes of our weather in all seasons of the year."[18] Oliver Goldsmith used the same term to point to a profounder condition, one of unaccountable anxiety, and Anne, countess of Winchilsea, in her best-known poem, entitled "The Spleen," wrote of it as a "Proteus to abus'd mankind, / Who never yet thy real cause could find, / Or fix thee to remain in one continued shape." Among its protean variations are enumerated, "panic fear" and "stupid discontent," and of it she writes that:

> Thro' thy black jaundice, I all objects see,
>   As dark and terrible as thee,
> My lines decried, and my employment thought
> As useless folly, or presumptuous fault.[19]

Although Lady Winchilsea felt the search for "its mysterious ways, / Too deep for human thought," the Quaker Matthew Green was more typical of his age in placing reliance on a muscular optimism to put matters right:

> To cure the mind's wrong bias, Spleen,
> Some recommend the bowling green;
> Some, hilly walks; all, exercise; . . .
> Laugh and be well.[20]

"Spleen-fogs," as he called the attacks, would be dissipated easily enough, he was sure, by a simple bucolic life, one free from ambition and enthusiasm. (Fear of enthusiasm was to the eighteenth what fear of cholesterol is to the late twentieth century.) Perhaps it was for that reason that the English failed to take the spleen seriously, even though some of them were prostrated with what was referred to vaguely as "gout in the head." The "white melancholy" from which Thomas Gray, the poet, suffered during his sojourn at Pembroke College, Cambridge,[21] differed only in color from the "black dog" that attacked the Elder Pitt. Both of these were from time to time engulfed in unutterable and irresistible torpor, in total mental paralysis.[22] It is of course possible that such a drastic onslaught as this had largely, or even purely, somatic origins. On the one hand, however, they do seem novel, and on the other, the boredom of spleen assumes for the first time on record a generality in society that made one of Steele's characters in the *Spectator,* early in the century, declare that "every heavy wretch who has nothing to say excuses his Dulness by complaining of the Spleen."[23]

Whatever the origins of these conditions, a contemporary sufferer in France, Madame du Deffand, who presided for forty years over the most brilliant salon in the kingdom, maintained that she had the "terrible misfortune to be *born* subject to ennui."[24] She distinguished, as had La Rochefoucauld, between the boredom brought on by external conditions and the qualitatively different form that they both perceived as arising from within. "I always have three or four companions with me. . . . They do not entertain me in the least," she wrote, "but I can stand *this* type of boredom better than solitude."[25] However, with few exceptions, "everybody is bored . . . and it is this detestable ennui that pursues everybody . . . that sets everything in motion."[26] But she also recognized it as the intimation of ultimate nullity—"ennui is a foretaste of nothingness, but nothingness is preferable to it."[27]

This insistent sense of nothingness, of the void, the abyss, and the associated sense of hollowness and loss that permeated her letters struck notes that were fundamental to the chord of boredom. They established a natural harmony between her and Voltaire, who found "ennui the worst of all conditions,"[28] and who spoke of his métier as being "the abyss of eternal nothingness." All his efforts were spent trying to keep boredom at bay, but to no lasting avail.

Moving into the early nineteenth century, the eponymous hero of Sénancour's *Obermann* hits the note more firmly in his question, "Why has the earth lost its charm for me? I no longer feel any satisfaction, everywhere I find the void," and in a letter that he writes later in the book he refers to the first day "when I became aware of the void that surrounds me."[29]

This world-weariness appears to have been regarded at least as early as 1766 by the English as a particularly Gallic state of mind, for in a letter of the earl of March of that year there occurs the sentence, "Your last letter was the most cheerful I have received from you, and . . . without that d——d French bore," and the Oxford Dictionary has a reference to another letter of that year in which 'bore' is paired with 'French.'[30] No etymological explanation is provided there, or elsewhere, for the addition of the new meaning of the word 'bore' in the mid–eighteenth century,[31] nor has the first appearance of its derivative 'boredom' in the middle of the following century been in the least accounted for by the lexicographers: its arrival is recorded without comment. The eminent English philologist, Logan Pearsall Smith, identified 'bore' as an eighteenth-century neologism that, like many others in preceding and succeeding periods, was untraceable with any certainty to a word of previous formation.[32] He made the valuable observation later in the same work that 'interesting' first appeared in print within two years of 'bore', and that both belong to what he called "the curious class of verbs and adjectives which describe not so much the objective qualities and activities of things as the effects they produce on us."[33] From the historical survey thus far it is clear that many, if not all, elements of the mental state existed before the term itself but, as Smith put it, "when anything becomes important to us it finds its name."[34] The new term was evidently needed to give focused expression to a malaise that had increased in such degree, incidence, and reflective awareness, that it now called for a new, exact, vernacular form to replace or to substitute for the alien and only narrowly available *ennui,* and the always somewhat literary 'spleen', both of which were within a relatively short time displaced by the newcomer. There is much evidence, as will become apparent, that what Gabriel Marcel said of the introduction of the notion of 'value' into philosophy holds true also of the extended, or new, meaning taken on by 'bore', namely that "the idea and the word together make their appearance as the marks of a kind of internal collapse, and what the word really seeks to indicate is the place where the collapse has taken place."[35]

The nature of the "collapse," and of the forces leading to it will be examined later, but its origins are to be found in earlier centuries, so that the actual coining of a new word, or perhaps the addition of a new sense to the old one, was a belated recognition of a fait accompli, rather as the American War of Independence, or the French Revolution, gave only apparently sudden and surprising expression to what were in fact disjunctions between social and political realities that had been developing for decades. Perhaps the best explanation for the new arrival lies in Benjamin Whorf's perceptions that "language . . . is in some sense a superficial embroidery upon the deeper processes of consciousness," and that "language, through lexation [the giving of names to parts of the whole manifold of experience]" makes the speaker "more acutely conscious of certain dim psychic sensations."[36] One might liken the process to that in which a quite long-term, vague uneasiness, may suddenly become sharply focused into "pain-in-the-stomach," and in being recognized actually becomes something different from the previous blurry state.

It took the acute sensibility of a Wordsworth to recognize, at least in some measure, what was going on, and had been going on for some time. In his preface to *Lyrical Ballads* he wrote prophetically, a herald of an unrecognized present truth, a forecaster of a future development:

> For a multitude of causes, unknown to former times, are now acting with a combined force to blunt the discriminating powers of the mind, and, unfitting it for all voluntary exertion, to reduce it to a state of almost savage torpor.[37]

That the phenomenon derived from some alteration in the culture of western Europe rather than from some national peculiarity or from innate psychological dispositions is clearly established by the geographical scatter of its leading spokesmen and victims in the nineteenth century: the Dane Kierkegaard, the Russians Dostoevsky and Tolstoy, the Germans Nietzsche and Schopenhauer,[38] the Swedes Ibsen and Strindberg, the French Chateaubriand, Flaubert, Sainte-Beuve, Gautier, Baudelaire, Verlaine, and Mallarmé. Each was, as it were, a seismograph whose individual tracings pointed jointly to the seat of a cultural upheaval that has shaken the foundations of Western civilization: long and slow in its genesis, sudden and violent in its irruption. As men of genius they were far more acutely aware of the fundamental shift of which boredom, it is true, is only one indication, but, as Kierkegaard wrote,

> how ruinous boredom is for humanity . . . Boredom is *the root of all evil*. Strange that boredom, in itself so staid and stolid, should

have such power to set in motion. The influence it exerts is altogether magical, except that it is not the influence of attraction, but of repulsion. [Emphasis added][39]

Kierkegaard may have been the first to have pointed to the active, destructive form that boredom can take, though Stendhal, writing of the burning of Moscow as "le plus bel incendie du monde," gave an early hint of it. In the Dane's recognition there lies an indication of a watershed—perhaps *the* watershed—in European culture. He also clearly perceived that it was not idleness that led to boredom. "Boredom," as he wrote,

> is the root of all evil. . . . Idleness is not an evil, indeed one may say that every human being who lacks a sense for idleness proves that his consciousness has not yet been elevated to the level of the human. There is a restless activity which excludes man from the world of the spirit, setting him in a class with the brutes, whose instincts impel them always to be on the move.[40]

There is a strong link between this insight and the medieval view that sloth and restlessness, the inability to enjoy leisure, are intimately related to acedia. The latter meant, as Josef Pieper so well expressed it, that

> a man renounces the claim implicit in his human dignity. In a word, he does not want to be as God wants him to be, and that ultimately means that he does not wish to be what he really, fundamentally, *is*.[41]

Acedia is, in this view, identical with that "despair from weakness" which Kierkegaard analyzed as the "depairing refusal to be oneself."[42]

One catches a clear resonance of Cassian's understanding of the monk's frantic desire to escape ("aversion from the place, boredom with one's cell") in Kierkegaard's observation that

> everyone who feels bored cries out for change . . . One tires of living in the country and moves to the city; one tires of one's native land, and travels abroad; one is *europamüde,* and goes to America, and so on; finally one indulges in a sentimental hope of endless journeyings from star to star.[43]

The first major expression in English of this form of boredom occurred in Byron's *Don Juan,* published in 1819. Perhaps through his familiarity with the French literary scene, he accepted the Continental view of England, as in Tocqueville's phrase, "la patrie du spleen," but he pointed to the lack of an English word for it:

> For *ennui* is a growth of English root,
> Though nameless in our language; we retort
> The fact for words, and let the French translate
> That awful yawn which sleep cannot abate.[44]

For Byron's hero (and, it seems, for his creator), "the world's a game; Save that the puppets pull at their own strings . . . There's little left but to be bored or bore."[45]

Dickens appears to have been the first to make literary use of, if he did not actually coin, the word 'boredom' for a state of mind that on his side of the Channel evolved immediately from an emotion lacking an English label to the "chronic malady of boredom" endured by Lady Dedlock in *Bleak House*.[46] 'Borism', a form that did not survive, was apparently current a generation earlier, but however fleeting its existence is further proof of a mood on the way up.[47]

Invention and usage of these new terms suggest the development of some new social reality, but the manifestations of it in the British Isles—or at least in England—tended to be morose, sullen, phlegmatic, and generally private, in contrast with the forms it assumed on the Continent, where it had fast become fulminating, virulent, and destructive. Kierkegaard recognized the power and dynamism that could lead one to "find oneself driven by the demoniac spirit of boredom deeper and deeper into the mire, in the very attempt to escape."[48] A similar fear of the effects of boredom afflicted Dostoevsky, who also shared Kierkegaard's dread of the "sins of reason," ('reason' here in the sense of *ratio* rather than *intellectus*), and "so-called objective truth." He was not, however, so much concerned, or perhaps even aware, that boredom was already a powerful presence as he was fearful of its spread when the mathematicians had the world to their liking, a world of "progress" represented by what he called the "Crystal Palace". "Man," he wrote,

> has always been afraid of this mathematical certainty . . . He feels that when he has found it there will be nothing for him to look for. But of course there is no guaranteeing (this is my comment) that it will not be, for instance, frightfully dull then (for what will one have to do when everything will be calculated and

tabulated), but on the other hand everything will be extraordinarily rational. Of course boredom may lead you to anything. It is boredom sets one sticking gold pins into people.[49]

It is the boredom of certainly that he fears, and he would no doubt have agreed with Kierkegaard who saw it as his task to "create difficulties everywhere."[50]

But, as it appears to have been the French who first as a whole society had experienced boredom, so it was in France in the nineteenth century that there occurred the most numerous and most exact expressions of the plague. Flaubert is the best contemporary witness to the novelty of the condition:

> Connaissez-vous l'ennui? non pas cet ennui commun, banal, qui provient de la fainéantise ou de la maladie, mais cet *ennui moderne* qui ronge l'homme dans les entrailles et, d'un être intelligent, fait une ombre qui marche, un fantôme qui pense. [Emphasis added][51]

He is also the first, to distinguish explicitly between what one might call 'simple' boredom *(ennui commun, banal)* and what will henceforth in this study be referred to as 'hyperboredom', what he styles "modern boredom." The delineation of the exact characteristics of these two distinct states will be undertaken later. It may be enough for now to distinguish between feelings of tedium that are at least in principle conscious responses to specific irritants that tend to goad one into escape ('simple' boredom), and a deep-seated agony, scarcely realized except by its effects, which is brought on by an all-inclusive, persisting perception of what is taken to be one's existential situation ('hyperboredom'). In the simple type, there is a temporary discomfort in the midst of an existence that is usually congenial, or at least possessed of meaning; in hyperboredom, there is a more or less complete withholding of assent to existence, positively or negatively. The former one might liken to seasickness: acutely distressing and all-encompassing while the cause persists, almost immediately and quite harmlessly ended with the removal of the cause. The latter would be comparable to an agonizing and chronically painful disease, possibly incurable, in some cases ending in death.

Sainte-Beuve, in the same decade as Flaubert, recorded Chateaubriand's lifelong sufferings from the inroads of hyperboredom and the latter's perception of it not just as a personal affliction but as a disease of pandemic proportions:

Je crois, disait-il [Chateaubriand] que je me suis ennuyé dès le ventre de ma mère. Il a comme engendré cet ennui incurable, mélancolique, sans cause, si souvent doux et enchanteur dans son expression, sauvage et désséchant au fond, et mortel au coeur, mortel à la bonne et saine pratique familière des vertus,—le mal de René, qui a été celui de notre age, maladie morale . . . Le voilà donc à sa source cet ennui qui va s'épancher à travers le monde, qui cherchera partout l'infini et l'indéterminé, le désert.[52]

To Sainte-Beuve it seemed, however, that having reigned for fifty years, more or less, it had, by this time, "à peu près disparue . . . du moins n'est plus endémique." Théophile Gautier at about the same time pointed to another aspect—the world-weariness of its victims:

Tous les ennuie, tous les excède, tous les assomme; ils sont rassassiés, blasés, usés, inaccessibles. Ils connaissent d'avance ce que vous allez leur dire; ils ont vu, senti, éprouvé, entendu tout ce qu'il est possible de voir, de sentir, d'éprouver et d'entendre.[53]

But it is without doubt Baudelaire who most acutely captures the morbid richness of *l'ennui moderne*. He, too, points to the blankness of the state and to its sweeping extent: "L'Ennui, fruit de la morne incuriosité / Prit les proportions de l'immortalité."[54] This is only one facet of Baudelaire's many-sided experience and expression of boredom, for he is in himself one of the great prophets of the malady. In the very first poem of *Les fleurs du mal* he elevates it above every other vice:

(parmi)
Les monstres glapissants, hurlants, grognants, rampants,
Il en est un plus laid, plus méchant, plus immonde!
Quoiqu'il ne pousse ni grands gestes ni grands cris
Il ferait volontiers de la terre un débris
Et dans un baîllement avalerait de monde;
C'est L'Ennui[55]

There is a certain irony, in view of the French association with 'bore' in the eighteenth century, in the fact that Baudelaire felt he had to import the word 'spleen' into the French language to do justice to the exalted quality of his own ennui, and at the same time as the neologism 'boredom' was being introduced into English!

In *Les fleurs du mal*, boredom seems suddenly to emerge with all its modern characteristics: intense, desperate, agonized, undirected irritation alternating with a sullen, morose, lowering lethargy and an utterly exasperated violence.[56] Nerves are stretched, it seems, beyond the breaking point—but for no definite, identifiable reason—and hence beyond the reach of any conceivable salve. Baudelaire gives a picture of unequaled clarity of the hyperbored, self-immured victim-torturer, realizing as a result of his travelings that the world is "une oasis d'horreur dans un désert d'ennui," and that in consequence, "Nous voulons, tant ce feu nous brûle le cerveau / Plonger au fond du gouffre, Enfer ou Ciel, qu'importe? / Au fond de l'Inconnu pour trouver du *nouveau*."[57] Anything new or unknown to escape the acid in the brain;[58] any abyss, however infernal, to escape the horror— "n'importe où, hors de ce monde."[59] The outburst in *Le nain jaune* of 3 October 1867, the year of his death, comes as no surprise:

> Je m'ennuie!!! Elle m'ennuie!!!! Tout m'ennuie!!!!! L'ennui est, dit-on, la maladie commune, un mal chronique qui ronge notre génération entière, et dont les plaisirs artificiels du moment ne la guériront.[60]

All values are reversed, and in the words of Baudelaire's commentator,

> le spleen du poète veut que cette transformation s'effectue dans le pire sens, puisque, à ses yeux, l'or se change en fer, le paradis en enfer, et certain au delà celeste en une sorte de cimetière, de nécropole.

From this state of mind, as Léon Bopp points out, it is no distance to nihilism, to Nothingness, to the Void.[61]

That the affliction was not confined to men of letters can be gathered from the career of Napoleon III. As Louis Napoleon he had become president of the Second Republic set up after the 1848 Revolution, whose outbreak was itself attributed by Lamartine to the fact that France as a whole was bored. "La France," as he said, "s'ennuie." As emperor, Napoleon brought that boredom to an imperial measure: "Tout lui pèse. Il se lève ennuyé, il passe sa journée, il se couche ennuyé."[62]

Railing against the actual, or impending, boredom of existence, in the individually differing manner of Baudelaire, Kierkegaard, or Dostoevsky, was actually less novel than the negativism that had evidently quite hollowed out its first, and certainly unsurpassed, "husk-man," Bartleby the Scrivener, the eponymous antihero of Melville's short story, "pallidly neat, pitiably respectable, uncurably forlorn," responding to all requests "in a singularly mild, firm voice, 'I would prefer not to.'"[63] He was the forerunner of a series of such humanly empty characters, of which the protagonist of Camus's *The Stranger* is a more recent and eminent example, someone so bored that he can muster no more than a trifling and transient interest in the speech of the prosecutor in his own trial for murder: "The only things that really caught my attention were occasional phrases, his gestures and some elaborate tirades—but these were only isolated patches."[64] The somnambulistic, semi-anasthetized, semi-selfed Meursault's view of the world raises echoes of the Marquise du Deffand and her references to visitors who "me paraîssaient des machines à ressort," clockwork automatons. The myth of the machine is heavily implicated, a world without human spirit in which, as E. M. Forster has Miss Quested say, "Everything exists, nothing has value."[65]

The inclusion of Melville is an indication that the dynamic New World was not proof against the affliction; it suggests that any simple equation between the affliction and a supposed fin de siècle effeteness in Europe is quite wide of the mark.[66] This thought occurred to an least one American writer who, in the 1880s, gave it as his opinion that Schopenhauer had been the first

> to detect and logically explain that universal nausea which, circulating from one end of Europe to another, presents those symptoms of melancholy and disillusion which, patent to every observer, are borne indubitably of the insufficiencies of modern civilization.[67]

Though inaccurate in several respects, as is clear from what has been written above, the comment is interesting both in its very early recognition of what was toward and for containing what seems to have been the first use in English of the word 'nausea' in relation to boredom.

Descriptions, analyses, diagnoses, and prognoses of boredom multiplied with the turn of the century, and from being mainly the preoccupation (and often the condition) of writers and philosophers, it now began to become the professional terrain of the social scientists—sociologists, psychologists, and economists. This development might be taken as reflecting no more than the emergence of these disciplines were it not for the fact that the theme gained ever-increasing prominence in its original fields.

It was the French sociologist Emile Durkheim particularly who took it upon himself to explain in terms of social science how, in an individual,

> a thirst arises for novelties, unfamiliar pleasures, nameless sensations, all of which lose their savour once known . . . from now on nothing remains behind or ahead of him to fix his gaze on . . . he cannot in the end escape the futility of an endless pursuit.[68]

He might almost have been paraphrasing his compatriot Baudelaire in his most erethistic mood, in the language of his own specialty, when he wrote of the man of his times (the 1890s) that "he aspires to everything and is satisfied with nothing."[69] He saw men of his era as afflicted by a "marked desire for the infinite," and considered that

> suicides of both types suffer from what has been called the disease of the infinite . . . In one, thought, by dint of falling back upon itself, has no object left; in the other, passion, no longer recognizing bounds, has no goal left. The former is lost in the infinity of dreams, the second in the infinity of desires.[70]

Although Durkheim was here primarily addressing the question of suicide, his analysis carried with it wide implications, as George Simpson emphasizes in his introduction to *Suicide:*

> Where the rate [of suicide] increases rapidly, it is symptomatic of a breakdown in the collective conscience, of a basic flaw in the social fabric. . . . Thus suicide for Durkheim shows up the deep crisis in modern society, just as the study of any other social fact would.[71]

The application of his analysis to hyperboredom will be considered later. While Durkheim did not himself explicitly connect suicide and boredom, Alvarez treats self-destruction in a larger historical perspective and observes that in the latter half of the eighteenth century, "the polite response to the act was a yawn, and even those about to die went through the motions of indifference." He goes on to quote Horace Walpole's reaction to the news of a suicide: "It is very provoking that people must always be hanging or drowning themselves or going mad"; commenting that "that mixture of aristocratic boredom and irritation is the typical eighteenth century note."[72] Flaubert struck a nineteenth-century note in recollecting how he and his friends had "lived in a strange world . . . we swung between madness and suicide; some of them killed themselves, another strangled himself with his tie, several died in debauchery in order to escape boredom; it was beautiful!"[73]

In Nikolai Stavrogin, Dostoevsky brought together boredom, nihilism, madness, and self-destruction. "I could have hanged myself out of boredom," the hero of *The Possessed* confesses, "and if I didn't it was because I was still hoping for something, as I have hoped all my life . . . I found life so boring it drove me mad."[74] And yet, in the very last sentence of the book, Dostoevsky very carefully states that "after the autopsy all our medical experts rejected any possibility of insanity."[75] It is society that is mad so far as he is concerned, and he would have seen largely eye to eye with Durkheim in perceiving that some kinds of madness and suicide are the diverse results of one cause—a disordered society, an anomic collectivity—a society without order and unable, because of its normative disintegration, to bring under control what Lewis Mumford calls man's "disordered subjectivity."[76]

The connection between boredom and suicide is most clearly visible in the protagonist of Mikhail Artzybasheff's nihilist novel, *The Breaking Point*, first published in 1915. In an analysis of this profoundly pessimistic book, Glicksberg remarks that "Cornet Krause suffers from acedia: The curse of indifference. Cherishing no illusions, drained of hope, infernally bored, he broods constantly on the idea of taking his own life."[77] Krause himself, just before putting the barrel of his pistol into his mouth and pulling the trigger, declares in front of his fellow officers that to him

life is not a tragedy, nor a horror, nor a senseless episode, but merely uninteresting. Nature and beauty are so trivial, one gets so tired of them. . . . love is so petty . . . humanity—simply foolish. The mysteries of the universe are impenetrable, and even should one fathom them it would be just as dull as before. Everything is as uninteresting as what we already know. In eternity there is nothing either small or large, and therefore even a match is a mystery and a miracle . . . but we know the match and it is uninteresting. And it's the same with everything. In the same way God would be tedious if we could see Him. Why have a God at all? It's superfluous.[78]

To move from the heated violence of a Baudelaire and the icy indifference of Artzybasheff's characters to the situation in the United States is to move from the torrent to the spring, from the developed to the emerging condition. In the 1930s, Elton Mayo was exercised about "those exaggerated demands which Durkheim described," arising, as he supposed, from the fact that "the problem of social disorganisation, with its consequent anomie, probably exists in a more acute form in Chicago than in other parts of the U.S."[79] In referring man's inner state to the economic structure, Mayo—and Durkheim—were, of course, on the same track as Marx (at least the earlier Marx), though neither he nor they expressly referred to what they might have regarded as no more than an epiphenomenon of the economic system—boredom.

There appears to be a paradox, or perhaps a contradiction, in this ascription of boredom to the understimulation of the factory worker on a production line, for earlier comments have pictured it in the light, rather, of a product of satiety, whether of appetite, of sensation, or of certainty, so that, as in the Midas myth, the gift of what one most desired and lusted after does not, when achieved, either nourish or delight. That the paradox or contradiction is more apparent than real and that boredom is no mere superficial derivative will be established later, but some confirmation of this may be found in a very different sort of work, one that appeared two years after the Hawthorne Studies. To the author of *Being and Time,* Martin Heidegger, boredom is such a fundamental mood that it raises, in the words of the title of the first chapter of his *Introduction to Metaphysics,* "The Fundamental Questions of Metaphysics":

Why are there essents rather than nothing? . . . The question is upon us in boredom, when we are equally removed from joy and despair, and everything about us seems so hopelessly commonplace that we no longer care whether anything is or is not.[80]

To Georges Bernanos, also writing in the 1930s, boredom appeared through the eyes of his country priest not only as fundamental but as omnipresent and overwhelming:

The world is eaten up by boredom . . . you can't see it all at once. It is like dust. You go about and never notice . . . But stand still for an instant and there it is, coating your face and hands . . . the world has long been familiar with boredom . . . such is the true condition of man. No doubt the seed was scattered all over life, and here and there found fertile soil to take root; but I wonder if man has ever before experienced this contagion, this leprosy of boredom; an aborted despair, a turpid variety of despair that, without a doubt, is like the fermentation of a decomposing Christianity.[81]

And boredom continues to burrow deeper, a psychic black hole drawing man's energies, man's hopes, man's very sense of himself into an annihilating vortex, acting as an entropic force cooling and then freezing all aspiration, all ambitions, all sense of human being. Even despair is too positive an emotion to be fired by the exhausted indifference that renders ordinary boredom too much of an effort. Kafka was scarcely able to drum up enough will to write of his feelings of "absolute indifference and apathy." He felt himself to be

A well gone dry, water at an unattainable depth and no certainty it is there. Nothing, nothing . . . The present is a phantom state form. . . . Nothing, nothing. Emptiness, boredom, no, not boredom just emptiness, meaninglessness, weakness.[82]

Half a century later, Beckett's *Waiting for Godot* was a virtual celebration of stasis. The stage business is set out in elaborate detail in the stage directions, choreographing the almost nothing that happens all the time, so that boredom becomes the main point of interest. Saul Bellow might very well have had *Godot* in mind when he wrote that "imagination has even tried to surmount the problems of forcing boredom itself to yield interest," and it is surely a sign of the times that the play has never ceased to draw audiences. Life seems to have come to be seen as pointless as a slow bicycle race in which the aim is to get as near as possible nowhere for as long as possible. Sisyphus in our own time no longer needs or possesses the psychic energy to deal with a hill and a stone: why bother? Who *needs* it? In another of Beckett's plays, *Happy Days*, constant ridiculous business (busy-ness, in fact) is used to underline his belief that the human alternatives are suffering and boredom. In his book on Proust he writes that

the pendulum oscillates between two terms: Suffering—that opens a window on the real and is the main condition of the artistic experience, and Boredom—with its host of tophatted and hygienic ministers, Boredom that must be considered as the most tolerable because the most durable of human evils.[83]

Considering mankind's prospects from a very different perspective, Teilhard de Chardin saw boredom as "the great enemy of the modern world, 'Public Enemy No. 1' . . . Mankind is bored. Perhaps this is the underlying cause of all our troubles."[84] Certainly almost every major writer in the twentieth century has dealt with it, and many have dwelt upon it, but the crucial question is, of course, Just where does it arise from and what does this almost obsessive concern mean and portend? Rollo May, writing over twenty-five years ago from his experience as a clinical psychologist, maintained that "while one might laugh at the meaningless boredom of people a decade or two ago, the emptiness has for many now moved from the state of boredom to a state of futility and despair," and, one would now have to add, far beyond, even to nausea, disintegration, and to the terrifying situation in which even "evil itself bores."[86]

It may be emblematic that it should be precisely in an American best-seller of 1975, *Humboldt's Gift*, that the leading character is occupied in putting together a group of studies on "Great Bores of the Modern World," on the ground that "from the beginning mankind experienced states of boredom but that no one had ever approached the matter front and center as a subject in its own right."[87] Though the present study was begun two years before Bellow's novel appeared—an interesting example of the *Zeitgeist* at work—its intention is to approach the subject in just the way Bellow's protagonist proposed. It will not be possible, however, for the writer to say, as does Charles Citrine, "I saw that I had stayed away from problems of definition. Good for me. I didn't want to get mixed up with theological questions about *accidia* and *tedium vitae*."[88] As may already be apparent, such matters as definition and 'theological' questions are quite unavoidable.

As a pendant to this introductory chapter, and to meet the possible objection that too much is being made of a condition that is no more than an existential queasiness affecting only the effete spirits of intellectuals and aesthetes, it may be worth quoting from an article printed in *Reader's Digest* a few years ago. The article was headed "How to Cope with Boredom," and it read in part:

> Despite its extraordinary variety of diversions and resources, its frenzy for spectacles and its feverish pursuit of entertainment, AMERICA IS BORED. The abundance of efforts made in the United States to counter boredom have defeated themselves, and boredom has become *the disease of our time*.[89]

NOTES

1. George Gordon, Lord Byron, *Don Juan*, Canto 13, Stanza 95, lines 7–8.

2. Cf. the perceptive comment of Erich Fromm that "the danger of the past was that men became slaves. The danger of the future is that men may become robots. True enough, robots do not rebel. But, *given man's nature*, robots cannot live and remain sane, they become Golems, they will destroy their world and themselves because they cannot stand any longer the boredom of a meaningless life" (*The Sane Society* [Greenwich, Conn.: Fawcett Books, 1955], p. 313).

3. From *a-*, "not"; *kedos*, "care."

4. Cassian, *De institutis coenobiorum*, bk. 10. Quoted in Helen Waddell, *The Desert Fathers* (London: Constable, 1946), pp. 157–59.

5. Ps. 119:28.

6. "Our evidence shows plainly that these two notions—spiritual inappetence and laziness—co-existed as integral elements of the vice, not only during the Scholastic period, but indeed from at least Cassian's *Instituta* on. Their mutual relation is nothing more than that between a state of mind (*taedium* or *tristitia* in the Scholastic sense) and external faults which flow from its effects (expressed as *otiositas*) and covering sleepiness, roaming, and later all sorts of negligence" (Siegfried Wenzel, *"The Sin of Sloth": Acedia in Medieval Thought and Literature* [Chapel Hill: University of North Carolina Press, 1967], p. 174).

7. Geoffrey Chaucer, "The Parson's Tale," in *The Works of Geoffrey Chaucer*, ed. F. N. Robinson (Boston: Houghton Mifflin, 1957), pp. 249–50.

8. *De remediis utriusque fortunae*, 2. 93. 183. Wenzel goes so far as to declare that "Petrarch secularized the vice" (*"The Sin of Sloth,"* p. 186).

9. Raymond Klibansky, Erwin Panofsky, and Fritz Saxl, *Saturn and Melancholy: Studies in the History of Natural Philosophy, Religion and Art* (London: Nelson, 1964), p. 221, n. 25. The lack of any evident reason for the affliction makes it possible to chart its persistence and spread to a more generalized population. Two centuries after Petrarch's time, in a physician's handbook, there occurs a telling reference to "a kind of dotage without any feuer, hauing for its ordinarie companions, fears and sadnes, *without any apparent occasion.*" Du Laurens, Andre, *A Discourse of the Preservation of the Sight: of Melancholike Diseases; of Rheumes, and of Old Age*, tr. Richard Surphlet (London, 1599, emphasis added.) Cited in Lawrence Babb, *The Elizabethan Malady* (East Lansing: Michigan State University Press, 1951, p. 38).

10. Robert Burton, *The Anatomy of Melancholy* (London: J. M. Dent & Sons, 1932), p. 390.

11. C. D. du Cange, *Glossarium Mediae et infimiae Latinitatis* (Paris: Firmin Didot fratres, 1840–50). I, 51: VII, 442. Cited in Edward Peters, "Notes Toward an Archaeology of Boredom," *Social Research* 42 (1975): 500.

12. Cotgrave, *A Dictionarie of the French and English Tongues* (London, 1611). Cited in Peters, "Notes," 507.

13. Letter to Sir H[enry] G[oodyer?], 4 Oct. 1622 in Edmund Gosse, *The Life and Letters of John Donne* (Gloucester, Mass.: Peter Smith, 1959), vol. 2, p. 169.

14. John Donne, "The Calme," *The Complete Poetry of* John Donne, ed. John T. Shawcross (Garden City, N.Y.: Doubleday, 1967), lines 50–55.

15. Blaise Pascal, *Pensées* (Baltimore: Penguin Books, 1966), pp. 69–70.

16. Loc. cit.

17. Ibid., p. 147.

18. George Cheyne, *The English Malady.* Cited in Oswald Doughty. "The English Malady of the Eighteenth Century," *The Review of English Studies,* 2 (1926), p. 259.

19. *Minor Poets of the Eighteenth Century,* ed. Hugh l'Anson Fausset (London: J. M. Dent & Sons, 1930), pp. 101, 103.

20. Ibid., p. 211.

21. Gray mentioned his own condition in a letter of 1757: "I am alone and ennuye to the last degree, but do nothing" (*Correspondence of Thomas Gray,* vol. 2, ed. Paget, Toynbee, and Whibley [Oxford: Oxford University Press, 1935], p. 520).

22. Cf. "Spleen . . . affection connue chez nous sous la dénomination de maladie noire "(*Dictionnaire de la conversation* [1875], quoted in Guy Sagnes, *L'ennui dans la littérature française de 1848 à 1884* [Paris: Lib. Armand Colin, 1969], p. 61).

23. Cited in Reinhard Kuhn, *The Demon of Noontide: Ennui in Western Literature* (Princeton, N.J.: Princeton University Press, 1976), p. 139.

24. Marquise du Deffand [Marie de Vichy-Chamrond], *Lettres de la marquise du Deffand à Horace Walpole* (Paris: Lib. de Firmin Didot Frères, Fils & Cie, 1864) Vol 1, Letter 96 (19 December 1770), p. 293.

25. *Lettres de la marquise du Deffand,* Vol 2, Letter 213 (21 February 1775), p. 108. (emphasis added). As she added a little later in the same year, "Variety is good in everything, even to changing one's brand of boredom," Letter 218 (8 April 1775), p. 121.

26. *Lettres de la marquise du Deffand,* Vol. 1, Letter 110 (1 May 1771), p. 340.

27. Ibid., Letter 335 (8 October 1779), p. 390.

28. Cited in R. Kuhn, *Demon of Noontide,* p. 151.

29. Etienne Pivert de Sénancour, *Obermann: Lettres publiées par M. . . . Sénancour,* nouvelle edition (Grenoble: Arthand, 1947), 1:5. "*Ennui*—'le mal d'Obermann,' as it came to be called" (H. G. Schenk, *The Mind of the European Romantics* [New York: Frederick Ungar Publishing Co., 1966], p. 57).

30. *Oxford English Dictionary,* 1933, s.v. bore." The French, however, saw it as peculiar to England. In a letter to Sophie Volland of 18 October 1760, Diderot wrote of "le spleen ou les vapeurs Anglaises" (Sagnes, *L'ennui dans la littérature française,* p. 62). Evidently this was still the view in Denmark well into the nineteenth century, for Kierkegaard remarked that, so far as boredom was concerned, "the English are the paradigmatic nation" (Sören Kierkegaard, *Either/Or* [Princeton, N.J.: Princeton University Press, 1944], p. 286).

31. There is no reference to the word 'bore' with this meaning in *Johnson's Dictionary,* but it is of interest to find Johnson quoting Sir John Evelyn as having remarked a full century earlier that "we have hardly any words that do so fully express the French *clinquant, naïveté, ennui*" (*Johnson's Dictionary,* 1756 ed., s.v. "Bore").

32. Logan Pearsall Smith, *The English Language* (London: Oxford University Press, 1966), p. 50.

33. Ibid., p. 128.

34. Ibid., p. 131.

35. Gabriel Marcel, *Man against Mass Society* (Chicago: Henry Regnery Co., 1962), p. 170.

36. Benjamin Lee Whorf, *Language, Thought & Reality,* ed. John B. Carroll (Cambridge: The M.I.T. Press, 1964), pp. 239, 267. As E. H. Gombrich rather neatly paraphrases Whorf's thought, "language does not give name to pre-existing things or concepts so much as it articulates the world of our experience" in *Art and Illusion* (Princeton: Princeton University Press, 1969), p. 90.

37. William Wordsworth, *Wordsworth and Coleridge: Lyrical Ballads, 1798,* ed. H. Littledale (Oxford: Oxford University Press, 1911), preface, p. 230. Cf. "I lost/ All feeling of conviction" (*The Prelude,* 11).

38. Schopenhauer is actually something of an exception within the ranks of the bored, ennui bringing in his case withdrawal rather than protestation. His moroseness outdid anything British (their boredom being, like many another of their activities, that of the inspired amateur), as the following from *The World as Will and Idea* demonstrates: "We are fortunate enough if there still remains something to wish for and to strive after, that the game may be kept up of constant transition from desire to satisfaction, and from satisfaction to a new desire, the rapid course of which is called happiness, and the slow course sorrow, and does not sink into that stagnation that shows itself in fearful ennui that paralyses life, vain *yearning without a definite object*, deadening languor" (Arthur Schopenhauer, *The World as Will and Idea* [London: Kegan Paul, Trench, Trübner & Co., 1906], 1:215, emphasis added).

39. Kierkegaard. *Either/Or*, p. 281.

40. Ibid.

41. Josef Pieper, *Leisure: The Basis of Culture* (New York: Random House, 1963), p. 38.

42. Sören Kierkegaard, *The Sickness unto Death* (Garden City, N.Y.: Doubleday & Co., 1955), p. 187.

43. Kierkegaard, *Either/Or*, p. 287. The "sentimental hope" does not seem so sentimental in this day and age, and the contemporary equivalent of boredom driving us from our cell is its driving us, at least in our daydreams or vicariously, from our planet or even from our galaxy. It might, of course, drive one down into oneself, with perhaps better chance of remedy.

44. George Gordon, Lord Byron, *The Works of Lord Byron*, ed. E. H. Coleridge (New York: Octagon Books, 1966), vol. 6, *Don Juan*, canto 13, stanza 101. It is amusing to see the French mirror-version of this, expressed half a century later: "le spleen (un autre mot intraduisible peut-être parce que la chose qu'il exprime est un produit tout anglais)" (*Le monde illustré*, 14 September 1861, quoted in Sagnes, *L'ennui dans la littérature Française*, p. 44).

45. Byron, *Don Juan*, canto 13, stanza 89, canto 14, stanza 18.

46. Charles Dickens, *Bleak House* (New York: W. W. Norton & Co., 1977), p. 350.

47. Michael Scott, *Tom Cringle's Log* (London: J. M. Dent & Sons, 1915): "Borism is fast attaining a head it never reached before" (p. 401).

48. Kierkegaard, *Either/Or*, p. 287.

49. Fyodor Dostoevsky, *Notes from the Underground*, in *The Short Novels*, trans. Constance Garnett (New York: Dial Press, 1945), p. 145.

50. Sören Kierkegaard, *Concluding Unscientific Postscript* (Princeton, N.J.: Princeton University Press, 1968), p. 166.

51. Gustave Flaubert, *Correspondance*, vol. 1 (Paris: Conard, 1926–33), 151, letter to Louis de Cormenin, 7 June 1844. A recognition occurs in the writing of Emile Montégut, a friend of Baudelaire's, of the shift in the nature of ennui from its being at the beginning of the nineteenth century "presque une religion, . . . une noble inquiétude" to its becoming within a generation a sickness that kills the soul, and makes of "le néant" the soul's supreme hope and final reward (Charles Baudelaire, *Les fleurs du mal* [Paris: Ed. Garnier Frères, 1961], notes, p. 261). Elsewhere, Montégut gives voice to the conviction that "ennui is no longer an uneasiness, as it was in the time of Goethe and Rousseau, it is a negation. . . . Everything is receding, everything is becoming pale and corrupted, even despair, even ennui. . . . The human soul now derives its happiness from its impotence and places its supreme hope and ultimate recompense in nothingness" (R. Kuhn, *Demon of Noontide*, p. 329).

52. Charles Augustin Sainte-Beuve, *Chateaubriand* (Paris: Ed. Garnier Frères, 1948), pp. 81–82.

53. Théophile Gautier, *Mademoiselle de Maupin* (Paris: Ed. Garnier Frères, 1966), p. 31.

52. Baudelaire, *Les fleurs du mal*, "Spleen," p. 79. Auden, with his usual sharpness of perception, saw that *accidia* and boredom were synonymous: "Trim dualistic Baudelaire/ Poet of cities, harbours, whores/Acedia, gaslight and remorse" (W. H. Auden, *The Collected Poetry* [New York: Random House, 1945], p. 271). Further on in "New Year Letter, 1940," in the person of the poet, he also tied modernity and boredom together: "Baudelaire went mad protesting/That progress is not interesting" (ibid., p. 303).

55. Baudelaire, *Les fleurs du mal*, p. 6.

56. The first part of *Les fleurs du mal* is entitled "Spleen et idéal," and there are four separate poems at various points in the collection, each simply headed "Spleen." One senses a kind of hierarchy: 'Spleen' comprising *Ennui* in the singular among other miseries, *Ennui* in turn comprehending particular *ennuis*.

57. Baudelaire, *Les fleurs du mal*, "Le voyage," p. 159–60.

58. Isaiah Berlin marvelously well analyzes the "corrosive scepticism" of Tolstoy, for which the Russian word *netovschchik* was coined, and maintains that "what oppressed Tolstoy most was his *lack of positive convictions* . . . Nevertheless he longed for a universal explanatory principle," though he came more and more to suspect that "no core or unifying principle would ever be discovered" (*The Hedgehog and the Fox* [London: Weidenfeld & Nicholson, 1953], pp. 36–37).

59. The man in Kafka's story, "The Departure," acts under a similar compulsion. When he hears a distant trumpet, he mounts his horse, and when stopped at the gate by his servant and asked where he is off to, he replies that he does not know, "just out of here, just out of here. Out of here, nothing else, it's the only way I can reach my goal." "So you know your goal?" his servant asks. "Yes," he replies, "I've just told you. Out of here—that's my goal" (Franz Kafka, "The Departure," in *The Complete Stories*, ed. Nahum N. Glatzer [New York: Schocker Books, 1971], p. 449).

60. Sagnes, *L'ennui dans la littérature française*, p. 77.

61. Léon Bopp, *Psychologie des "Fleurs du mal"* (Geneva: Lib. Droz, 1969), p. 640.

62. *Revue de Paris,* 1 July 1897, quoted in Emile Tardieu, *L'ennui: Etude psychologique* (Paris: Lib. Felix Alcan, 1913), p. 166.

63. Herman Melville, *Bartleby the Scrivener,* in *Five Tales* (New York: Dodd, Mead & Co., 1967), pp. 11–12. Melville seems to have coined a word of his own for hyperboredom (or perhaps just for boredom), 'hypos', which occurs on the first page of *Moby Dick.*

64. Albert Camus, *The Stranger* (New York: Random House, Vintage Books, 1946), p. 124.

65. E. M. Forster, *A Passage to India* (New York: Harcourt, Brace & World, 1952), p. 149. It is of interest that this sense of brute existence within cosmic nothingness that suddenly overwhelms Forster's heroine so that "she lost all interest" is immediately followed by the comment that "Miss Quested and Aziz and a guide continued the *slightly tedious expedition*" (emphasis added).

66. In response to the question which forms the title of his article, "Who Invented the *Mal de Siècle?*" Armand Hoog effectively disposes of the idea that the 'mal' was limited to *one* century, but then falls into the error of asserting that the tag was "the sign of a moral crisis that extended from 1740 to 1840"! "Not the 'mal de siècle,' but the 'mal des deux siècles.'" He remarks elsewhere in his article that "it is thus entirely justifiable to see in Baudelaire the last [*sic*] representative of the mal de siècle." Scarcely! (Armand Hoog, "Who Invented the *Mal de Siècle?*" in *Yale French Studies* 13 (1954), pp. 42–51.

67. Edgar Evertson Saltus, *The Philosophy of Disenchantment* (Boston: Houghton Mifflin, 1885), p. 160.

68. Emile Durkheim, *Suicide* (Glencoe, Ill.: Free Press, 1951), p. 256.

69. Ibid., p. 271.

70. Ibid., p. 284.

71. Ibid., p. 6.

71. A. Alvarez, *The Savage God* (New York: Random House, 1972), pp. 166–167.

73. Quoted ibid., p. 204.

74. Fyodor Dostoevsky, *The Possessed* (New York: New American Library, 1962), pp. 418, 427.

75. Ibid., p. 693.

76. Lewis Mumford, *The Pentagon of Power* (New York: Harcourt Brace Jovanovich, 1964), p. 370.

77. Charles I. Glicksberg, *The Literature of Nihilism* (Lewisburg, Pa.: Bucknell University Press, 1975), p. 104.

78. Mikhail Artzybasheff, *The Breaking Point* (New York: B. W. Heubsch, 1917), p. 306.

79. Elton Mayo, *The Human Problems of an Industrial Civilization* (New York: Macmillan, 1933), p. 159. These reflections derive from a series of studies that Mayo and his Harvard colleague, Fritz Roethlisberger, carried out at the Hawthorne plant of the Western Electric Company in Chicago, of the relationship between conditions at work and productivity.

80. Martin Heidegger, *An Introduction to Metaphysics* (Garden City, N.Y.: Doubleday & Co., Anchor Books, 1961), pp. 1–2.

81. Georges Bernanos, *The Diary of a Country Priest* (Garden City, N.Y.: Dell Publishing Co., Delta Books, 1956), pp. 295–96.

82. *The Diaries of Franz Kafka* 1914–1923 ed. Max Brod (New York: Schocken Books, 1949), p. 126.

83. Quoted in Ronald Hayman, *Samuel Beckett* (New York: Frederick Ungar Publishing Co., 1973), pp. 92–93.

84. Pierre Teilhard de Chardin, *The Future of Man* (London: Fontana, 1964), pp. 150–51.

85. Rollo May, *Man's Search for Himself* (New York: Dell Publishing Co., Delta Books, 1953), p. 24.

86. Georges Bernanos, *Oeuvres romanesques* (Paris: Gallimard, Bibliothèque de la Pléiade, 1961), p. 1469.

87. Saul Bellow, *Humboldt's Gift* (New York: Macmillan, 1975), p. 199.

88. Ibid.

89. Judson Gooding. *Reader's Digest*, February 1976, p. 51 (emphasis added).

2 • The Third Boredom

Man is bored not only when there is nothing to do, but also when there is too much, or when everything waiting to be done has lost its luster.

Geoffrey Clive

To feel bored is to suffer, in however slight a degree and for however short a duration. That is to say, it is a state of being from which one would like to be set free, from which one seeks relief even, perhaps, with desperation. Erich Fromm goes so far as to write that "one of the worst forms of mental suffering is boredom, not knowing what to do with one's self and one's life."[1] Numerous expressions such as "bored to death," "a crushing bore," and "out of one's mind with boredom" testify to its oppressiveness. From the state there often arises a peculiar kind of physical restlessness: children wriggle, move about almost randomly; adults may literally writhe as in agony, or merely fiddle, fidget, jitter, wander about aimlessly, yawn and stretch, run their hands through their hair, scratch themselves, peer about distractedly seeking any diversion or any object, eat compulsively and without appetite, or chain-smoke. In some instances of boredom (those which might be labeled 'normal'), these attempts at relief may be relevant in the degree that they do in fact lead to some activity that helps. But even in relation to these, some (particularly yawning, stretching, and scratching), seem somewhat absurd efforts to escape from a mental state by physical means, boredom being experienced as an incubus. The gaping mouth and the stretching limbs strongly suggest a physical attempt to expel, and yet since there is nothing to expel in any physical sense, the muscular contractions take on symbolic force, as if the organism were trying by some sympathetic magic to shake off the invisible load.

In boredom's simplest manifestation, it is quite possible to identify just what it is that is boring. Perhaps it is having to listen to a tale already heard (though children often delight in such retelling,

42

which makes it clear that repetition, per se, is not boring),[2] doing a familiar task for the Nth time, or having to be immobile. Or it may be the frustration of an entire life situation, the perception of a gulf between one's desire and the way (or the place in which or the person or persons with whom) one is forced to live. Such instances constitute a major category of boredom: that in which the source is readily recognizable. There is no difficulty in establishing this, for when the specific irritant is removed—the story is broken off, a new task is provided, one's interlocutor takes a yawn as a cue to change the subject—boredom vanishes,[3] just as seasickness immediately subsides when foot is set on dry land. Whatever one was being subjected to failed to interest, producing a sensation of interior opposition, of being forced widdershins, against one's grain.[4]

In this sense it is often regarded as inevitable, so much so that its occurrence in school is perceived by many adults as a useful part of their children's preparation for life, and by those same children as a normal and largely unavoidable accompaniment of their days in the classroom. Writers and artists have sometimes taken a more positive view of the state. Nietzsche, for example, wrote of it as *necessary* for "thinkers and all sensitive spirits" to whom, as he saw it, "boredom is that disagreeable 'windless calm' of the soul that precedes a happy voyage and cheerful winds."[5] In the last two decades it has been invested with still greater positive worth, at least for the "creative man" who, as Saul Steinberg is quoted as declaring, "is led, directed and controlled by boredom," and for whom "avoiding boredom is one of the most important purposes."[6] One art critic went so far as to divide the work of the 1960s into "high-boredom and low-boredom art," and, after referring to the creation by Andy Warhol of "the fiction of an autolobotomized euphoria in which repetition and boredom are prime values," carried on to give it as his opinion that "far from having no content, boredom is a state of potential richness, a desert that is now being irrigated and colonized."[7] The American anthropologist Ralph Linton suggested an even more sweeping significance for boredom, positing it as the force behind man's entire cultural development. "It seems possible," he wrote, "that the human capacity for being bored, rather than man's social or natural needs, lies at the root of man's cultural advance."[8]

Moravia's novel, *La Noia*, is basically concerned with boredom in the third sense detailed below, but it is illuminating in the present context because in the novel the main character distinguishes his own sufferings from boredom in this sense from those to which his father had been subject. He says that his father had,

> it was true, also suffered from boredom: but in him this suffering had been dissipated by happy wanderings in one country after another; his boredom, in other words, was the *ordinary kind of boredom* that asks no more than to be relieved by new and unusual sensations. [Emphasis added][9]

At other times, however, it may be difficult—even impossible—to identify the cause of the boredom. Children and adolescents are particularly apt to be attacked in this way, and their lamentations on the theme "I don't know what to do," "there's nothing to do," or "everything's a drag" are often accompanied by a resistance to all suggestions for relief: a strange masochism. In their case, the problem is frequently brought on by being unable to engage in something they would enjoy doing, a lack of some specific activity, or the unavailability of someone whose absent casts a pall over life, or through their ignorance of what they could do that *would* be interesting. In these situations, it is not that the cause of the boredom is unknowable, rather that, at least to the victim, it may not at the moment be known or if known, be capable of being dealt with; the situation is, however, at least in principle remediable.

These types of boredom—to be referred to from now on as boredom$_1$ and boredom$_2$—pose no conceptual problem. They are quite explicable in terms of a model of man that postulates his actions as deriving their dynamic from a store of undifferentiated 'energy' that drives him to engage with the world, to be in constant interaction with it, but in no particular way, much as hunger impels a man to eat, but not to eat especially this or that. Since the indifference or distaste is only for some detail or combination of details of existence, it needs no more explanation than does the fact that a particular individual may not like carrots or the color yellow.

But what of that other kind of boredom in which all people, objects, relations, and activities are permanently, and it seems unaccountably, stripped of interest, and in which the search for anything of interest itself appears utterly uninteresting, worthless, or totally ineffective? The victims of this affliction become prey for no discernible reason to indifference, apathy, lethargy, torpor, total nonvolition, affectlessness, or subject to an active *counter*volition, a desire to be free from some indefinable incubus, some corrosive irritant. There is an affect, but it is an affect without effectiveness in locating the source of the trouble.

There is at first glance a striking difference between the passive inappetence most thoroughly and convincingly incarnated in Ivan Goncharov's hero Oblomov and the active, desperate, tortured restlessness of those who feel desire of a sort, but desire not *for* anything in particular, but rather against everything available.[10] They desire, as Baudelaire wrote, to be "n'importe où, hors de ce monde," anywhere else just so long as it is *not here.* Robert Adams, in discussing the leaden inactivity of Oblomov, distinguished that worthy's state from "boredom [which] is properly an active sense of something not happening or not relating, a tension which blossoms ultimately into something like anguish,"[11] but Oblomov's character is in fact a subtle study of the essential ambiguity and contradictoriness of the two elements of acedia, *otiositas* and *tristitia,* decked out in mid-nineteenth-century Russian garb. Goncharov portrays him as subject at varying points in his story both to an anesthetized sloth and to a profound and painful sense of loss, the former eventually drowning out the latter. The mysteriousness of the forces at work are so perceptively teased out and are still, well over a century later, so illuminating and apropos that Oblomov's reflections on his state are worth quoting at some length:

> It grieved and hurt him to think that he was undeveloped, that his spiritual forces had stopped growing . . . he felt as though a heavy stone had been thrown on to the narrow and pitiful path of his existence . . . he was painfully conscious that something fine and good lay buried in him . . . it was as though the treasures bestowed on him by the world had been stolen from him and hidden in the depths of his own soul. Something hindered him from flinging himself into the arena of life and using his will and intellect to go full speed forward. It was as though some secret enemy had laid a heavy hand on him . . . The forest around him and in his mind grew thicker and darker . . . clear consciousness wakened more and more seldom . . . his mind and will had been paralyzed.[12]

And when he is bidden by his friend to rouse himself, he replies that he has tried, but without success; "and now . . . why should I? There is no inducement, my heart is at rest, my mind is sound asleep."[13] But it is not just he who is asleep, for despite the apparent liveliness of people in Saint Petersburg society, he perceives

> the boredom of it! Where is the real man in all that? . . . What does one find in it?—Intellectual interests, genuine feeling?

There is no center round which it all revolves, there is nothing deep, nothing vital. All these society people are dead men, men fast asleep, they are worse than I am! What is their aim in life? . . . all their life long they are asleep as they sit there . . . they are bored[14] (emphasis added).

It is no doubt this bipolar quality of acedia/boredom that has obscured the identity of its origin, leading to the suggestion recently made by Willard Gaylin that two terms, 'ennui' and 'boredom', are needed to apply respectively to the passive and active forms, because of the difference in their emotional tones.[15] However, what is in question is not the experience of boredom—the subjective and variable component arising from the temperament and life history of the individual—but the general factor or factors that give rise to the fundamental similarity sufferers from either of these forms share: their common and persisting inability to locate any object or pursuit of desire. In some, the failure takes the form of a withdrawal in varying modes and degrees into themselves, ranging from the good-humored indolence of Oblomov or the gentle melancholy of Verlaine to the virtual catatonia probably not existing in the pure state outside the person of Bartleby the Scrivener. In others, it becomes what Joyce styled a "kinetic emotion," throwing them into a harsh and determined resistance, as with Flaubert and Gautier; an embittered but articulate despair, as with Leopardi; or into the abyss of nothingness, as with Mallarmé, Huysmans, and Maupassant. Inasmuch as they cannot be accounted for in terms of the 'energy' model suggested above, all will for heuristic purposes be regarded as constituting a third boredom, for which a new term, 'hyperboredom', will be used from now on, both for ease of reference and because it has the advantage of accentuating the peculiar intensity that characterizes it in all its forms.

This discrimination among three mental states commonly subsumed under 'boredom' (a classification finally reducible to two, since $boredom_1$ and $boredom_2$ are alike in their ultimate 'relievability') runs counter to the tendency, especially among French commentators, to confuse the whole issue by endlessly dividing and subdividing. Jankélévitch, for example, refers to boredom as, variously, "protéiforme," "uniforme," "multiforme," "informe," and "difforme,"[16] and a commentator on this lavish and internally contradictory array of qualifiers uses its very profusion to support her claim that it is "un mal qui se réfuse au diagnostic."[17] That it "resists diagnosis" is at best an opinion, and one that it will become evident the present writer does not share. As against this obfuscation, a distinguished compatriot of Bouchez's, Paul Valéry, sees the matter differently. In referring to *ennui*, he is at pains to point out that he does not have in mind "l'ennui passager, ou l'ennui dont on voit le germe, ou celui dont on sait les bornes," but "cet ennui parfait, ce pur ennui, cet ennui qui n'a point l'infortune ou l'infirmité pour origine, et qui s'accommode de la plus heureuse à contempler de toutes les conditions."[18] The enigmatic nature of the malaise that attacks even those who are in "the happiest of conditions" (reminding one of the unfortunate Madame du Deffand's "ver solitaire," the solitary worm, as she called the ennui that gnawed at her spirit despite the outward luxury of her life) is heightened by the fact that the distractions and diversions that are customarily resorted to in order to banish it still carry with them the connotations of their Latin origins: *dis-trahere* ("to draw away") and *dis-vertere* ("to turn aside"), and raise the questions, "From what?" and "From whom?" and "Why are they needed?" and "Why do they fail?" 'Amusements' derives from the Latin *ad-musare* ("to idle"; Middle English 'idel', "void, empty"), and together with 'pastimes' suggests a sense of pointlessness and vacuity of living that seems to call for some explanation. Because 'boredom' has too often been taken to be just that—a single, undifferentiated phenomenon—it has largely escaped notice that there is a form of it that is not simply *more* of the same, to be eliminated by finding the right releaser, but a form that is sui generis.

Considering the inroads it has made in the last two centuries, it is strange how little has been written on the etiology of *any* kind of boredom. There is much description in literature and autobiography, and almost as much complaint, but there has been very limited penetrating examination of whence it arises. The earliest extended clinical treatment of the topic seems to be that of Otto Fenichel in 1934. He drew a distinction between 'normal' (or 'innocent') and 'pathological' forms, starting out from an earlier definition, that of Thomas Lipps, dating back thirty years, to the effect that it was "ein Unlustgefühl aus den Widerstreit zwischen dem Bedürfnis intensiver psychischer Betätigung und dem Mangel der Anregung dazu, bzw. der Unfähigkeit, sich dazu anregen zu lassen."[19] He was not satisfied with this definition, as it lumped together what to him seem clearly to be disparate mental conditions merely on the basis of superficially common symptoms, and so he went on to add "man weiss nicht *wie* man sich betätigen soll oder will,"[20] thus recognizing that the mood may be more than a temporary and contingent disconnection between our need for activity and our ability to know of any desirable outlets, any cathexis, any (as he styles them) "Abführhilfe," aids to discharge. In such instances he remarks that one is justifiably bored ("dann langweilt man sozusagen mit Recht"). Boredom in these cases is caused by externals—by the presence, or the absence, of particular people, objects, events, or processes—and the situation is one in which one might remark "nicht ich langweile mich, es sind die anderen die mich langweilen."[21] It can in principle, then, be relieved by a change in external circumstances, although neither we nor anyone else may actually know in advance what will bring relief.

But what if *nothing* will bring relief? In that case the boredom is, to the psychiatrist, 'pathological'. The situation brings to mind that of Tantalus, but with this alteration: that all objects of desire should not only withdraw as soon as he stretches out for them, but should become physically and psychologically invisible with the onset of desire; the longings are made even more excruciating because they cannot even be identified. The problem then becomes not just the absence of a desired outlet for an impulse, or the presence of undesired ones, as in the 'normal' state, but the nagging desire for *something,* the nature of which is forever hidden. Tantalus, although tormented with desire, is now unable to identify it, as in the myth, with the water in which he is immersed or the juice-filled fruit hanging over his head—he just . . . desires.

Fenichel explains this paradox by invoking the Freudian concept of 'repression'. Some instinctive aim has been driven out of sight, but pressure builds up in the "psychischer Apparat," a pressure increased by internal and external stimuli that lead to impulses, "Tendenzen die wieder die Spannungslosigkeit herbeiführen wollen." The state connoted by the word 'boredom' is that in which pressure or tension *fails to generate* "Triebimpulsen," so that adventitious stimulations are sought to release the pressure. As he states it, "Die Triebspannung ist da, das Triebziel fehlt," and this is accounted for by the fact that the ego is against the instinctual action the id desires, and hence disguises or eliminates awareness of the forbidden aim. There *is* an aim, but it is pushed out of reach of consciousness. The blasé, turned-off quietist and the obsessive activist represent the two extreme possibilities of the same damming up of the libido, *(Libidostauung);* boredom is au fond a physiological product manifesting itself physically, whether in restlessness or in torpor.[22]

Another Freudian, writing some twenty years later, posits a similar etiology and symptomatology:

> At the behest of the superego, certain instinctual aims and/or objects have to be repressed. This step results in a feeling of tension. At this point, if the ego has to inhibit fantasies and thought derivatives of these impulses because they are also too threatening, we have as a consequence a feeling of emptiness . . . as a kind of hunger . . . since the individual does not know for what he is hungry, he now turns to the external world with the hope that it will provide the missing aim and/or object. I believe that it is this state of affairs which is characteristic for *all* boredom. [Emphasis added][23]

A particular application of this theory is made by Leites in his analysis of Meursault, the central character of Camus's novel, *L'étranger.* The hero is in the grip of such profound boredom that his behavior has moved into a state referred to by Leites as "affect-lessness," the result of an indifference so great that to the magistrate's inquiry whether he regrets the murder he has committed he answers that "what I felt was less regret than a vague boredom" ("un certain ennui"). The text abounds in numbed expressions of indifference: "cela m'était égal," "tout cela se valait," "je n'attendais rien du tout," "il n'y avait pas d'issue," "cela revenait au même," "cela ne signifiait rien," "cela ne voulait rien dire." And Leites, cavalierly brushing aside Camus's own commentary on the meaning of his tale, and the general tenor of Camus's other work, proposes the theory that Meursault's boredom—and therefore Camus's own reasons for writing the story?—arose from repressed "murderous rage originally directed against the depriving parents," and that it is a defense against "the intense unconscious destructiveness."[24]

In the Freudian perspective, it is not actually boredom from which Meursault is suffering, but depersonalization, a state described by Edward Bibring as one in which people complain of "not having any feelings, of being blocked emotionally, being frozen, of feeling the self to be unreal, in a word, apathy."[25] He puts apathy, boredom, and depression in the same category, insofar as all are "affective states and states of mental inhibition." In depression, so much energy is needed to inhibit the aggressive (but forbidden) drive that the whole organism is drained of vitality. In boredom, the drive remains energetic but, as it were, anonymous, so that while its effect is felt, it cannot be gratified because its real objective, being forbidden and repressed, forever eludes identification. Depression is sharply differentiated from the other two members of the trio, not by the absence or camouflage of the drive, but by "the ego's shocking awareness of its *helplessness* in regard to its aspirations."[26] Repeated or traumatic failure leads to a suppression of the drive, with drastic effects on the ego.

Dino, the leading character in *The Empty Canvas*, is a good example of 'Freudian' boredom at work. He is portrayed as subject to a radical, boredom-producing, ambivalence—one that comes out in his relations with his mistress, whose image overlaps equivocally with that of his mother. Going through his mind as he waits for his mistress to appear is the thought that

> out of that door . . . would soon issue something which I desired at the same time to know and not to know, something for which I felt at the same time both appetite and disgust—Cecilia, or in other words, reality.[27]

'Appetite' stands for the oedipal desire that must be repressed; 'disgust', for the emotion that powers the repression barring the way to the forbidden consummation. This love/hate relationship with reality is a note that is struck at the very beginning of the novel and is linked throughout with boredom. "Boredom," Dino declares, "to me consists in a kind of insufficiency, or inadequacy, or lack of reality."[28] Moravia makes it clear later on that 'reality' is exactly what boredom is a shield against: "Boredom is the suspension of all relationship with reality."[29] Even the suffering of boredom is preferable to the reality that has been repressed. If he finds anyone he loves, he must reject her: "I *wanted* to become bored with Cecilia."[30] Reality (that is to say, truth) must be denied because it is too horrible, and reality is therefore attenuated by repression. This explains why Dino considers that "the feeling of boredom originates . . . in a sense of the absurdity of a reality which is insufficient, or anyhow unable to convince me of its effective existence."[31]

In Freudian terms, boredom is contingent, the result of a repression that bars the way to the discharge of tension, of a return to the nonpleasurable noninterest of the real and desirable emptiness; one is, in Milton's words, "calm of mind, all passion spent." But one psychoanalyst at least—Bergler—seems to entertain doubts, for in an article about what he calls "the disease-entity boredom (alysosis)," he writes, "Boredom is a universal problem, constantly threatening the psychic balance of the individual . . . Everyone has to find some specific remedy for the looming of the *sickness,* boredom" (emphasis added).[32] Although later in the article he retreats into a more involuted form of the classic position, he has said enough to suggest that there have intruded into his thoughts ideas akin to those of Pascal, some three hundred years earlier, and of many others since, that boredom in the nontrivial sense—hyperboredom, that is—is not a state induced in man by circumstances, upbringing, temperament, or some combination of all three, but is an innate, primal force within mankind:

> Man's condition. Inconstancy, boredom, anxiety[33] . . . Even if we felt quite safe on every side, boredom on its own account . . . would not fail to emerge from the depths of our hearts where it is naturally rooted, and poison our whole mind. Man is so unhappy that he would be bored even if he had no cause for boredom, by the very nature of his temperament.[34]

Bishop Bossuet, whose life overlapped that of Pascal, wrote in strikingly similar fashion:

> Encore que la vie fût exempte de tous les maux extraordinaires, sa durée seule nous serait à charge, si nous ne faisions simplement que vivre, sans qu'il mêlât quelquechose qui trompe, pour ainsi dire, le temps et en fasse couler plus doucement les moments. De là vient le mal que nous appelons l'ennui qui seul suffirait pour nous rendre la vie insupportable.[35]

In this view, the only things that can keep man from the torments of boredom are sufferings or powerful emotions of other sorts: pain,[36] fear, anger. These preoccupations will take his mind off the nullity of existence until age comes to soften the asperity.[37] His various torments will drain his energies and leave little or none to fuel his always incipient boredom. However, deprived as this may be of executive power for the moment, it is ever ready to revive when the diversions end, a fact that Schopenhauer recognized: "L'ennui est toujours aux aguets pour occuper le moindre vide laissé par le souci . . . Le besoin et la souffrance ne nous accordent pas plutôt un répit que l'ennui arrive."[38] Giacomo Leopardi similarly saw boredom as merely staved off by pains or pleasures. Life to him was a sort of vacuum that if left empty of sensation for even a brief moment would become occupied by ever-waiting boredom, which is

de la nature de l'air qui remplit tous les intervalles des choses
materielles et tous les vides de ces choses . . . De même tous les
intervalles de la vie humaine, entre les plaisirs et les douleurs,
sont occupés par l'ennui. . . . si elle est vide de toute joie et toute
peine, il faut qu'elle soit pleine d'ennui . . . La vie n'est qu'un
tissu de douleur et d'ennui.[39]

Kierkegaard was no less certain of the positive, dynamic force of
boredom, however unobtrusive it might seem. For him, "boredom
depends on the nothingness that pervades reality; it causes a diz-
ziness like that produced by looking down into a yawning chasm."[40]
Unlike Pascal, in whose eyes it was a certain consequence of man's
existential situation, Kierkegaard saw it as "partly an inborn talent,
partly an acquired immediacy."[41] There is nothing inevitable about
it, unless we choose to let it be so, or look for the wrong escape,[42] in
which case we fall into "the second form of boredom," the acquired
one: "If we *remain* in boredom as such, it *becomes* the evil principle; if we *annul* it, we posit it in its truth; but we can only annul
boredom by enjoying ourselves."[43] No such genial escape exists
from the point of view of Pascal or Freud. For the latter, boredom
is negative and accidental; for the former, positive and endemic;
for Kierkegaard, it is threatening but avoidable. Despite their
marked differences, all three explanations are open to the same
objection: that they fail to explain the growth of the phenomenon
in the last three hundred years. It may, of course, be argued that
the increase is more apparent than real, that the heightened attention to boredom in literature, of which numerous examples have
been cited, is itself a *literary* phenomenon. This would not, of
course, explain why writers should come to take such an increased
interest in it, but it would in any case run counter to the obvious
fact that writers are invariably and inevitably reporters of their
ages' concerns whether they intend to be or not, and that they are
read especially because, and in the degree that, they have the skill
to express in focused and refined form—and often ahead of the
general perception—the major preoccupations of their times. As
Alan Tate wrote some years back, "It is the business of the man of
letters to call attention to whatever he is able to see; . . . it is his
duty to render the image of man as he is in his time."[44]
One would seem justified, therefore, in accepting the change as
real, and this inevitably raises doubts about the universal, culturewide applicability of the Freudian explanation of the genesis of
boredom in the individual. Since no society is free of taboos, of

forms of behavior or thought prohibited under heavy psychic or physical sanction—in a word, of 'repression'—the presence of boredom should be common to and widespread, indeed well-nigh omnipresent, in all societies at all times, but particularly in those of a puritanical cast. But there seems to be no evidence that this is true even of recent Christian puritan communities; rather the contrary, in fact. 'Bored' just is not the word that springs to mind when one thinks of the extraordinarily moralistic and repressive zealots of the seventeenth century in England, of the followers of John Knox, of the Anabaptist communities of the preceding century, or of the Pilgrim Fathers setting out for the New World and surviving in the wilderness. One would more readily think of the latter days of the Roman Empire, a time of relaxed authority and weakened moral imperatives as an epoch of boredom. Nor does there appear to be any confirmation in the findings of the cultural anthropologists. Boredom is no more prevalent in harsh, restrictive societies than it is in genial, relaxed ones. In the one notable exception—the Ik—the boredom, significantly as it will be seen below, comes not from the presence of repression but from cultural disintegration.[45]

An analogous objection arises on the personal plane. If repression leads to boredom, why are we not *all* bored? And if it is answered that in some people sublimation is more successful than in others, one feels compelled to inquire what causes the supposed psychic mechanism to be less effective in dealing with the problem in some epochs than in others? It becomes clear that it makes no better sense to account for the phenomenon by invoking an explanation based on the fact of purely individual variations in a common human psychic structure, without regard to forces at work in any particular society at any particular point in time, than it would to try to account for the growing number of people killed on the roads on the basis of personal decisions and characterological factors, without regard to such nonpersonal ones as the increasing size and number of vehicles and roads, and of such at first glance unrelated matters as the use of alcohol and drugs.

Now, if a particular symptom increases to pandemic proportions, four explanations seem to be possible: (1) that the same cause or causes that previously led to only a few cases are now operating with greater force; (2) that the resistance of people to this cause or causes has somehow been weakened; (3) that some new cause or causes have come into play; or (4) that the symptom is only apparently the same. Of these, the first seems to be ruled out by the lack of evidence that repression has grown, a fortiori, since the indica-

tions point in the opposite direction, and an even cursory comparison of what Cassian, Pascal, Baudelaire, and any of the
psychoanalysts who have been cited have to say about the nature of
boredom and its effects would establish the identity of the symptoms beyond reasonable doubt, which rules out the last. In support
of the third, that some new cause is operating, are references by
such student/suffers of the malady as Gustave Flaubert and Emile
Tardieu to the phenomenon they referred to as *l'ennui moderne,*
modern not in respect of its manifestations but rather in relation to
its origins. It is one contention of this study that their observations
and intuitions are essentially correct and that there is indeed a
relatively new cause at work. This is to maintain that, alongside the
cases of boredom for which the Freudian explanation may well be
adequate, there are many for which it is not and for which some
other causal explanation is needed.

Of course, neither a new cause nor a different symptom can be
logically admitted when one turns to consider Pascal's account. For
him boredom arises from some force within man and is a given, but
that very fact renders his explanation incapable of accounting for
boredom's massive increase in modern times. If it is a constant in
man's nature as are, say, greed, lust, and envy, then what ground
is there for supposing that it, any more than they, should have
come from relative obscurity and rarity to striking prominence?
But it does seem possible to account for the change by means of the
second of the four possibilities mentioned above—that there has
occurred a weakening of man's resistance, more specifically that of
man in Western culture. In this view, there is in man an inherent
potential for boredom, indifference, or loathing, but no less for
involvement, enthusiasm, commitment, and delight. What de-
cides overall which of these potentials becomes effective is much
less the individual than the extrapersonal—social attitudes and
forces. The Pascals of the world are just those in whom the initial
potential is weighted on the side of boredom, and they project onto
mankind in general their own profound sense of dis-ease. From
this angle, in writing that "rest proves intolerable because of the
boredom it produces," Pascal is speaking for himself and not for
most, or perhaps even many, of his contemporaries. From what is
now known, however, it is possible to see him, not as an accurate
recorder of the actual condition of his fellow men of the seventeenth century, but as a prophet (an early-warning system, to put it
in modern terms), acutely sensitive to changes still so subtle and
undeveloped as to be quite invisible to and undetectable by the

vast majority of those around him at the time. A prophet is, after all, a forecaster of what is to come only in the sense that he is one who can see that it has already begun to happen. One is reminded of Rilke's lines: "Ohne unsern wahren Platz zu kennen,/handeln wir aus wirklichen Bezug./Die Antennen fühlen die Antennen."[46]

It becomes clear that there is a crucial inadequacy in both the Pascalian and the Freudian accounts of the genesis of boredom. The former psychologizes (or theologizes) it, while the latter is even more radically reductionist and makes it ultimately a matter of physiology. Neither has any sense of history, of social change and its effects on the individual in society; adherence to either as a general explanation would make any gross change in the incidence of boredom rationally inexplicable.[47] It is necessary to look further and deeper.

NOTES

1. *The Sane Society* (Greenwich, Conn.: Fawcett Books, 1955), p. 253.

2. This is the only sense in which the *OED* recognizes it: "To weary by tedious conversation, or simply by the failure to be interesting" (*Oxford English Dictionary*, 1933, s.v. "bore").

3. Lewis Mumford sees in this a cause of man's survival: "Man seems to have been saved by a special trait, still visible in infants and children—a positive need for repeating experiences, accompanied by equally positive delight in repetitive bodily movements and vocal expressions. Thus habit and custom and ritual restored the order man's excessive cerebral development, which divorced him from his instincts, had taken away" (*The Pentagon of Power* [New York: Harcourt Brace Jovanovich, 1964], p. 369). Julian Jaynes suggests another possibility: "We need some vestige of the bicameral mind [the mind-state he posits as existing before the development of the subjective consciousness, our former method of control] to help us. With consciousness we have given up those simpler, more absolute methods of control of behavior which characterized the bicameral mind. . . . *We know too much to command ourselves very far*" (*The Origin of Consciousness in the Breakdown of the Bicameral Mind* [Boston: Houghton Mifflin, 1976], p. 402, emphasis added).

4. This was evident over sixty years ago to Henri Le Savoureux, who wrote: "L'homme sain, qui ne dépense pas suffisamment tout son énergie disponible, s'ennuie; dès qu'il lui est permis d'employer ses forces, l'ennui disparaît" ("L'ennui normal et l'ennui morbide," *Journal de psychologie normal et pathologique*, 1914, p. 144).

5. Friedrich Nietzsche, *The Gay Science* (New York: Random House, Vintage Books, 1974), p. 108.

6. Robert Hughes, "The World of Steinberg," *Time*, 17 April 1978, p. 92.

7. Brian O'Doherty, *Object and Idea* (New York: Simon & Schuster, 1967), pp. 232–37 passim.

8. Ralph Linton, *The Study of Man* (New York: D. Appleton–Century, 1936), p. 90.

9. Alberto Moravia, *The Empty Canvas* (New York: Farrar, Straus & Cudahy, 1961), p. 10. "The Empty Canvas" is a curious translation of the novel's Italian title—*La Noia*—which literally means 'boredom'.

10. The hero of Moravia's novel cited above at one point remarks that "what struck me above all was that while I strongly wanted to do something, I had absolutely no wish to do anything in particular" (ibid., p. 16).

11. Robert Adams, *Nil* (New York: Oxford University Press, 1966), p. 235.

12. Ivan Goncharov, *Oblomov* (London: J. M. Dent & Sons, 1932), pp. 93–94.

13. Ibid., p. 171.

14. Ibid., pp. 177–78.

15. Willard Gaylin, *Feelings* (New York: Random House, Ballantine Books, 1980), pp. 111–13.

16. Vladimir Jankélévitch, *L'aventure, l'ennui, le sérieux* (Paris: Aubier-Montaigne, 1963), chap. 2 passim.

17. Madeleine Bouchez, *L'ennui* (Paris: Bordas, 1973), p. 7. An American author of a popular work on the subject, Bruce Leckart, makes the useful comment that "boredom . . . can *feel like* just about anything" and that "depending on the circumstances you may *feel* anxious, angry, depressed, tired, or any number of other unpleasant emotions." However, like Jankélévitch and Bouchez, he supposes that "boredom takes many forms," so that help depends on understanding your own particular kind of boredom at any particular time." He does later refer all boredom to "common *sources*," but sees these as "within ourselves" (Bruce Leckart, with L. G. Weinberger, *Up from Bordeom, Down from Fear* [New York: G. P. Putnam's Sons, Richard Marek Publishers, 1980], pp. 28, 31, 37).

18. Paul Valéry, *L'âme et la danse* (Paris: Gallimard, 1944), p. 163.

19. Otto Fenichel, "Zur Psychologie der Langeweile," *Imago* 20 (1934):270.

20. Ibid.

21. Attributed to Field Marshal Ligne (emphasis added). Cf. the remark by Moravia's hero: "In reality it was not that Cecilia was boring, it was I who was bored" (*Empty Canvas*, p. 101). Here the boredom is only *occasioned* by others; the cause lies within.

22. "Auf physiologischer Grundlage, aber, meinen wir, beruht die Langweile in beiden Fällen, nämlich auf der physiologischen Grundlage der Libidostauung" (Fenichel, "Zur Psychologie der Langeweile," p. 554).

23. Ralph R. Greenson, "On Boredom," *Psychoanalytic Quarterly* 21 (1952):19. Van Den Haag has much the same to say: "Repression bars impulses from awareness without satisfying them. This damming up always generates feelings of futility and apathy or, in defence against it, an agitated need for action. The former may be called listless, the latter restless, boredom" (Ernest Van Den Haag, "Of Happiness and Despair We Have No Measure," in *Mass Culture*, ed. M. Rosenberg [New York: Free Press, 1957], p. 534). For a more recent analysis of boredom along classic Freudian lines, see Haskell Bernstein. "Boredom and the Ready-Made Life," *Social Research*, 42 (1975), in which "chronic boredom" is described as a "specific psychopathological entity, the expression of an internal dysfunction." It is perceived as deriving from "the truly oppressive authority within which remains hidden," and the increase of which is attributed to an alleged post-World War II "tendency to start the training of children at a much earlier age." pp. 512–537, passim.

24. Nathan Leites, "Trends in Affectlessness," *American Imago* 4 (1947):101.

25. Edward Bibring, "The Mechanism of Depression," in *Affective Disorders*, ed. Phyllis Greenacre (New York: International Universities Press, 1953), p. 28.

26. Ibid., p. 39.

27. Moravia, *Empty Canvas*, p. 213.

28. Ibid., p. 3.

29. Ibid., p. 274.

30. Ibid., p. 278.

31. Ibid., p. 3. That Moravia is in fact transcending the Freudian view is perceptively

pointed out by his fellow countryman, Chiaromonte: "Moravia's boredom . . . is an inner condition that is both without a cause and chronic, that not only undermines the very possibility of experiencing different or changeable moods but also infects the external world, rendering it uninhabitable and inadequate, not by reason of this or that deficiency but taken as a whole and, almost, without repeal. At this point we pass from the 'physical' (and naturalistic psychology) to the 'metaphysical' (Nicolo Chiaromonte, *The Worm of Consciousness and Other Essays* [New York: Harcourt Brace Jovanovich, n.d.], p. 154).

32. Edmund Bergler, "On the Disease-Entity Boredom (Alysosis)," *Psychiatric Quarterly* 19 (1945):35.

33. Blaise Pascal, *Pensées* (Baltimore: Penguin Books, 1966), p. 24.

34. Bergler, "On the Disease-Entity Boredom," pp. 69–70.

35. Quoted in Emile Tardieu, *L'ennui: Etude psychologique* (Paris: Lib. Felix Alcan, 1913), p. 327.

36. In one of her letters, Mme. du Deffand wrote "si je n'étais pas un peu malade, je crois que je m'ennuierais beaucoup" (*Correspondance* [Paris: Calman Leon, 1867], letter of 1774, p. 203).

37. Tardieu cites Mme. de Maintenon, arrived at a vast fortune, as remarking that "je m'ennuie de vivre, je m'ennuie à la mort, je ne veux plus rien aimer au monde, ma seule consolation, c'est d'être vieille" (*L'ennui*, p. 140).

38. Arthur Schopenhauer, *The World as Will and Idea* (London: Kegan Paul, Trench, Trübner & Co., 1906), p. 327.

39. Quoted in Tardieu, *L'ennui*, p. 162.

40. Sören Kierkegaard, *Either/Or* (Princeton, N.J.: Princeton University Press, 1944), p. 287.

41. Ibid., p. 286.

42. To Pascal *any* attempt to escape through diversions was just an effort to escape from reality, from the nothingness of the individual that boredom expressed (see *Pensées* 36, p. 82; 414, p. 148).

43. Kierkegaard, *Either/Or,* p. 286.

44. Alan Tate, *The Forlorn Demon* (Chicago: Henry Regnery Co., 1953), p. 8.

45. Colin Turnbull, *The Mountain People* (New York: Simon & Schuster, 1972), chap. 10 passim.

46. Rainer Maria Rilke, *Sonnets to Orpheus* (Berkeley and Los Angeles: University of California Press, 1971), sonnet 12, part 1, p. 24. The translation in this edition is appalling (even allowing for the difficulties Rilke poses). The following seems to follow the sense of the lines: "Without really knowing the truth of our situation, we go on acting as if we did, but our antennae grope out for the messages in the air," and some (though this is my interpolation) are more finely tuned and more sensitive than others.

47. What Schacht says of alienation, a cognate state, would apply equally well to boredom: "One of the most striking features of the vast literature on alienation is its historical blindness" (Richard Schacht, *Alienation* [New York: Doubleday & Co., 1971], p. xxix).

3 • The Nature of Hyperboredom

Sensibility immensely more irritable . . . the abundance of
disparate impressions greater than ever . . . The tempo of this
influx *prestissimo* . . . A kind of adaptation to this flood of
impressions takes place: men unlearn spontaneous action, they
merely react to stimuli from outside. . . . *Profound weakening
of spontaneity.* . . . Artificial change of one's nature into a
"mirror"; interested but, as it were, merely epidermically interested.

Friedrich Nietzsche

the sin which believes in nothing, seeks to know nothing, in-
terferes with nothing, enjoys nothing, loves nothing, hates
nothing, finds purpose in nothing, lives for nothing, and only
remains alive because there is nothing it would die for.

Dorothy L. Sayers

If hyperboredom cannot adequately be attributed to repression or
to a 'natural' tendency in man, then just what does account for it
and, in particular, for its great increase in recent times? It seems
possible that the apparent problem is actually caused by a hidden
assumption—that one is bored because someone, something, some
situation, does not 'interest' one, so that boredom is considered to
be a state of noninterest. But if that were the case, the word
'uninterested' would surely be enough. On reflection, however, it
soon becomes clear that the emotional accompaniment of hyperboredom is by no means merely the simple opposite of 'interested',
a state of moderate or slightly irritated unconcern as against one of
moderate attraction. On the contrary, it is a state charged with
negative feelings, and it is far more accurate to equate it with a
state of strong *counter*interest (a "kinetic emotion," in Joyce's
words) and with a rejection of all available possibilities than with
mild aloofness or withdrawal. It is a state close to that which
Goethe has his Mephistopheles give voice to when he exclaims,
"Ich bin der Geist der stets verneint" ("I am the Spirit which always
denies"), always seeks to reduce to nothingness.[1]

Pure Oblomovism, the quietist form of hyperboredom, is not truly characteristic of our age. The constant adjurations that are exchanged when people meet and part— "Relax!" "Take it easy!" "Cool it!" "Go with the flow!" "Hang loose!" "No sweat!" "No problem!"—all have about them a submerged animus against 'up-tightness', an interested, energetic involvement, that was quite absent from the indolent Russian. The late twentieth century is a time not of Oblomovs and Bartlebys, but of people increasingly beset by hyperboredom's irritable, restless allotrope; of those who, like the Rolling Stones, "can't get no satisfaction." Half a century ago, the psychiatrist Otto Fenichel first drew attention to the kinship between boredom and anger in recording how one of his patients had described the hyperkinetic ennui that had brought him for treatment as "being angry," a state that with him was continual and that sometimes turned to blind rage.[2] More recently, another psychiatrist, Ernest Schachtel, pointed to the obvious— but previously unremarked—fact that, as *ennui* and *ennuyant* can mean either boredom or annoyance, each can mean *both together;* that in this ambiguity, "the intrinsic connection between boredom and anger finds expression."[3] He also underlined the centrifugal tendency of hyperboredom, writing that

> most people in our civilization, especially in their leisure time, live in constant flight from boredom which they barely manage to escape. If they did not escape it but really experienced it, it would assume the quality of a negative passion.[4]

By the same token, he bracketed "boredom and its relative, mild depression," inasmuch as, in both states,

> the world loses its valences to the degree that the person loses his interest and does not turn toward the world . . . he is unaffected by the objects around him no matter how varied, beautiful, ugly, stimulating, attractive, or repellent these may be. . . . The depressed and bored are incapable of allocentric as well as autocentric interest.[5]

Though anger may be a component of hyperboredom, and though the hyperbored may be 'depressed', there is however, an essential difference in each case, as some comments by yet a third psychiatrist, Edward Bibring, clearly and forcefully establish. He points to the fact that boredom (and depersonalization) do not involve the self-esteem of the sufferer, whereas in depression,

> the narcissistically important aims are perpetuated, but the narcissistic core of the ego, its self-esteem, is broken down, since the ego functions—which usually serve the gratification of the particular narcissistic strivings—appear to be highly inadequate, partly due to reality factors, partly due to internal reasons.[6]

The important distinction being made is between the lack of any satisfying goal (in the case of the hyperbored) and the temporary though often prolonged loss of capacity to believe in one's ability to *achieve* a desired goal (in the case of the depressed). It is not that the depressed find the world uninteresting or withdraw attention from it as do the passive hyperbored. Indeed, they may very well find it *too* interesting, be appalled at what they see and hear, and feel so ill-equipped to deal with it that they recoil from reality. In other words, the depressed feel *themselves* inadequate; the hyperbored experience *the world* as insufficient. Comparing like with like—chronic, psychotic depression with hyperboredom—it is in fact from the former that the sufferer can be and often nowadays is rescued, by direct, external intervention, whether in the shape of drug or electroconvulsive shock therapy, whereas, though the hyperbored may seek various forms of escape, these provide at most temporary relief. It is quite possible that chronic depression and perhaps even acute depression are biochemical in origin, and that the effect of the basically physical malfunction is to distort the perception of the "ego function," that is, the capacity to achieve what is desired. Various therapies in one way or another correct the imbalance, and the ego function is restored. The cure is, like the sickness, encompassed within the bounds of the individual. With hyperboredom, however, the causes are far more elusive and seem to extend out into the entire culture.

On the analogy of interest in food (hunger), boredom is the equivalent not of *non*hunger, but of *anti*hunger, indeed of a revulsion against the very idea of eating, a psychic anorexia. To many an Irishman, pasta does not mean food and is actively *dis*tasteful, while to Neapolitans in general, potatoes do not count as part of a meal (a *real* meal, at any rate) and are no less lacking in appeal. Upon a little reflection, it is not difficult to recognize that 'taste' and 'distaste' for particular foods are not qualities that inhere in the foodstuffs themselves; they are qualities projected upon them by individuals and groups.

So it is with interest and with its opposite, boredom, for which, significantly, the word 'disinterest' has become, despite the complaints of the purists, more and more frequently substituted, perhaps by unconscious analogy with 'distaste'. Each individual will have a distaste for this, that, or the other food, and each may be bored by something different. However, just as an involuntary distaste for all food whatsoever is a certain sign of disorder, since appetite is a natural and obviously essential aspect of being human (or even animal), so would boredom with things in general, for to seek out and to attribute meaning to people, objects, relationships, processes, and states are human characteristics, all the more remarkable for being largely limited to the species.

Because they have no intrinsic meaning or interest by and in themselves, things are boring. It is to this emptiness of things that Walker Percy is pointing when he writes of the landscape through which a commuter in New Jersey passes for the thousandth time that it "has all the traits of the *en soi*, it is dense, sodden, inpenetrable, and full of itself; it is exactly what it is, no more, no less, and as such it is boring in the original sense of the word."[7] It seems to be a source of active irritation for human beings to be confronted by what has no meaning or interest for them, to the extent that they may respond like the infant in the high chair who has something distasteful put on his plate—they may lash out or recoil, unless, of course they have been, as the phrase has it, 'well schooled' (of which more in chapter 6). One may be taught patience, but if it is overdemanded, then either the original interest may die out, leaving a dead spot in the psyche, or the interest may be forced underground and produce a type of *Ressentiment,* a poisoning of the wells, a "venomous mass," as Scheler called it, leading "when the repression is complete [to] a general negativism."[8] This form of repression can be distinguished from that which Freudians have postulated as the cause of boredom by the fact that it is externally and explicitly enforced and generally has no particular connection with "instinctive aims," at least as those are envisaged by Freudians. In any case, since all societies impose their vision of what is significant—very often even more thoroughly than does ours—once again this explanation of boredom, even though it may often be enough to account for $boredom_1$ and $boredom_2$ (which we have no reason to doubt are present in some measure in all human societies) fails to explain the *growth* of those two types of the phenomenon, and more especially of hyperboredom, in the last century or two.

The unboringness of things in general derives from their forming part of a humanly significant complex. We are informed by our culture, however advanced or primitive, of the range of the significant, of what set of particulars out of the myriad that are in some sense 'present' shall be perceived; which is to say that the world is sliced up variously from place to place and from epoch to epoch, but that, in whichever way the slicing is done, there is a coherence within each slice, an *episteme:* the cosmos is accounted for without remainder. 'Culture', in its anthropological usage, is precisely that term which covers all those ways of perceiving and acting upon 'reality' which a particular group has articulated into *its* reality. It is the individual internalization of the profoundest elements of culture that constitutes a fully integrated personality that, in the words of John Dewey, "can be built up only as a world of related objects is constructed."[9]

The general framework of relationship is the crucial provision of culture, and without it man can be no more than a member of the species *Homo sapiens,* bereft of any but his purely animal aspects. Though possessing all the physical requisites for speech, for example, he will be unable—and will remain unable—to voice anything more than grunts and snorts. For *Homo sapiens* to become Man it is as if some focus were required, in default of which nothing, humanly speaking, will be utterable, visible, audible, or even perhaps thinkable. It is apparently possible for a man to survive in the feral state, but if he does so it is purely as an animal embedded in an *Umwelt.* In the normal human state, he appears to be driven inexorably to seek and to attribute meaning, and it is therefore quite possible for him to end up living, to cite Dewey again, in "a divided world, a world whose parts and aspects do not hang together, which is at once a sign and a cause of a divided personality." But if he does, Dewey adds, and "when the splitting-up reaches a certain point, we call the person insane."[10]

This may happen as a result of individual disorder, some form of schizophrenia in which, whether because of chemical imbalance or because of psychic malfunction, the self becomes divided. But Dewey's analytic scheme positively invites the interpolation of another category, the 'mad,' the hyperbored, those for whom the present age has made available the altogether accurate statement that they are "bored out of their skulls." They are those who inhabit "a world whose parts and aspects" do not *themselves* "hang together," and who internalize in a perfectly normal fashion a non-normal world, and specifically a world that is abnormal because it lacks commanding norms, is without cogent meaning. They might be described as the societally or culturally, rather than the personally, insane. Just as C. Wright Mills refers to "structural immorality" as that kind of wrong action which forms part of the norms of an institution, so might this kind of insanity be referred to as "structural madness."[11]

Just who ought properly to be regarded as mad is the concern of much of the work of R. D. Laing, and he points out how

> the "normally" alienated person by reason of the fact that he acts more or less like everyone else, is taken to be sane. Other forms of alienation that are out of step with the prevailing state of alienation are those that are labelled by the "normal" majority as bad or mad.[12]

He later expands on this idea that normality is a matter of definition:

> From an ideal vantage point on the ground, a formation of planes may be observed in the air. One plane that is "out of formation" may be abnormal, bad, or "mad," from the point of view of the formation. But the formation itself may be bad or mad from the point of view of the ideal observer.[13]

Laing does not, however, get quite to the heart of the matter, for he posits as current alternatives only those of being sane in a 'mad' society—and alleged to be a madman—or mad in a mad society (one whose norms are inverted)—and alleged to be sane. But there is room for another possibility, that of being a 'sane' man in a *normless* society, that is, someone who is 'adjusted' to a moral and aesthetic void. These are the ones Mumford is referring to when he writes, "Now that the binding ties of habit, custom and moral code have been loosened, an increasing portion of the human race is going out of its mind."[14]

Not so much "going," perhaps, as being driven, being inducted into a "trained incapacity," as Thorsten Veblen once put it, being "unfitted by being fit with an unfit fitness," in the more recent words of Kenneth Burke.[15] The link with boredom is made by Alan Watts, who saw speculative philosophy, as known in the West, as "almost entirely a symptom of the divided mind," going on to write that "so long as the mind is split, life is perpetual conflict, tension, frustration, and disillusion. Suffering is piled on suffering, fear on fear, and boredom on boredom."[16]

Since man's being is simply unthinkable apart from his Being-in-the-world (or put another way, since man and the world are not independently specifiable), boredom and all other profound moods are not just 'subjective states', contingent feelings telling one solely about an internality. Naturally, if we are detached, thinking substances, our mood must be on the subject side of the assumed subject/object dichotomy, but in that case we are left without any explanation of the source of what Heidegger calls "real boredom," to distinguish it from a situation in which it is a particular something—a book, a movie, a person—that, as he says, "merely bores us." If it is not this object or that activity which can be identified as the source of our experience of measureless, indefinite indifference, then what is the datum that gives rise to it?[17] Is there in fact any such datum, or is the very quest based on a premise that diverts one from the true origin?

No solution can be found so long as the self/world dichotomy is maintained. Only if man is seen as *Dasein,* as a being whose essence is a function of his Being-in-a-world, can there be any resolution of the riddle, not only to the puzzle of the origin of this generalized *ennui,* but also to the conundrum of its apparently localized and recent virulence. Man viewed as *Dasein* is always man in a context, is indeed a definition of man precisely as Being-in-a-context. Generalized, persisting moods thus illuminate "the way we find ourselves." As Macquarrie puts it, a mood "is not just a subjective emotion but an appreciation from the inside, as it were, of the situation in which we find ourselves."[18] Barrett expresses the same thought when he says that "words like dread, fear, guilt and boredom are not merely mental figments, but . . . modes of man's Being-in-the-world.[19]

Mood can thus be seen to tell us not merely something about the *sein* but also, and more profoundly, something about the *Da,* the facticity. Mood is one way of coming to understand the facticity, a cultural oscillograph, one of the modes by which the *Dasein* is disclosed to itself and becomes apparent. Man, in being bored, is betraying something of the nature of *the* situation, not just *his* situation; he is also revealing how he is attuned to his environment. In the words of Heidegger, "A mood assails us. It comes neither from 'inside' nor from 'outside', but arises out of Being-in-the-

world,*as a way of such Being.*[20] As with anxiety, boredom in this
'real' sense has no special object. To cite Macquarrie again:

> It is not some particular situation that gets disclosed in anxiety
> (though it may well be a particular situation that arouses it on a
> particular occasion) but man's total situation as an existent
> thrown into a world where he is and has to be.[21]

Now, what Heidegger says of boredom he also says of all the other
affective states—joy, fear, anxiety, and so on. What needs to be
considered in relation to boredom is its at first rather mysterious
newness, at least as a general phenomenon. Chapter 1 sketched
boredom's very emergence *as* a mood, and as a growingly oppressive and widespread one in the last two centuries—something that
would not, of course, be possible for the other affective states.
Some explanation seems to be called for to account for what one
may with only a slight exaggeration refer to as the 'invention' of a
mood. Since it seems in the highest degree unlikely that there
should have been a major alteration of the human psyche in modern times, the alteration must be found elsewhere. If Heidegger's
contention that the 'self' and the 'world' are dialectical polarities
within Being is accepted, the historical emergence of boredom
ceases to be puzzling.

Man has always, in Heidegger's eyes, had to struggle to realize
his authentic self. "The self of everyday Dasein," he writes, "is the
'they-self', which we distinguish from the authentic self—that is,
from the self that has been taken hold of in its own way."[22] But
where this everydayness is closer to Being as perhaps it may be
proper to suppose it is in a contemplative community, or in cultures that are closer to the rhythm of nature, or when life is lived so
close to the edge of existence as to admit virtually no alternatives,
then the development of an inauthentic self is unlikely or impossible. Until very recently, everydayness has been, for the vast
majority of the population, quite overwhelming and has had the
enveloping reality of a struggle for sheer survival. It has been a
matter not so much of developing a 'they-self' as acquiring an 'itself', and in the degree that neither left any room for alternatives,
the self, embedded as it admittedly was in necessity, had an authenticity, an organic connection with Being, that Heidegger himself rather seems to overlook. With one's nose close to the soil,
fear, joy, and anxiety are certainly elements of the facticity, but

there is no room for hyperboredom. There *is* no alternative, no other realm of possibility; every grain of rice, every drop of water, every drain or saving of energy has meaning, significance, importance. Life may be appallingly hard, often boring, but never hyperboring.

In this light, it is no longer so difficult to explain why hyperboredom has in the past been the affliction of only a few. For most, the culture (whichever it might be) was authentic, in the sense that it was experienced as self-evidently true, real, and inevitable, and hence compelling. Only if training and leisure provide some distance from the sheer imperatives of existence can the question of authenticity arise and with it—boredom! And even then the question only arises for the few, and never indeed arises *consciously* for any *but* the few, since it is of such a fundamental nature that only the unusually sensitive and rational are open to its corrosive potency. For the vast majority, the tediousness of life is experienced as boredom$_1$ (or boredom$_2$), the common or garden variety that tends to afflict any leisure class, whether it be nobles at Versailles, Foreign Legionnaires suffering from *cafard* in the remote *casernes* of the Sahara, the well-to-do in czarist Russia, or the immature in Western culture today. Idleness quite obviously lies at the heart of this particular manifestation, and Lieutenant Tusenbach in Chekhov's *Three Sisters* may speak for all: "I never worked a single day in my life," he complains. "Everyone wanted to protect me from work." but he foresaw the storm that was even then arising, the storm that would sweep away "indolence, apathy, prejudice against work, and the corruption of boredom."[23] Society as a whole is not, as yet, under indictment for failing to provide meaning, only one's particular and potentially remediable position within it. Relief is seen as possible—even if only through revolution.

The question arises, as has been detailed above, even in a society still bearing all the external marks of authenticity, but here it was a psychological rather than a sociological phenomenon: it was from the hermit of the Thebaid that the meaning of everything had departed because he had succumbed to the lures of acedia, that fatal doubt of the certainty of God's existence, and of his purpose as a child of that God, passing through this world to the external joy of the Beatific Vision. The organizing principle of his whole being—of Being itself—had been shattered. In the dark night of the soul, nothing any longer had meaning to the shattered victim, but the culture, or subculture, still retained its coherence. Certainty had deserted man, not Man certainty.

But what if certainty does desert the culture? Is this not exactly what has progressively occurred in Western society, most clearly since Descartes, but surely as the result of a process with its origins far back in medieval times? If one of the prime functions of a culture is to provide meaning,[24] and if the incidence of boredom (the result of a conscious or unconscious realization of the collapse of meaning) greatly increases, then it is logical to conclude that there is something gravely amiss with the culture, something seriously disordered in the facticity at its deepest, least accessible level. Heidegger, writing of what he called the spiritlessness and dissolution of the psychic energies of the nineteenth century, attributed the trend to a profound shift, "prepared by earlier factors." He saw the shift as deriving from "the destroyed relation to Being," and, quoting from his earlier inaugural speech, made clear what he means by "the spirit":

> Spirit is neither empty cleverness nor ther irresponsible play of the wit, nor the boundless work of dismemberment carried on by the practical intelligence; much less is it world-reason; no, spirit is fundamental, knowing resolve toward the essence of being.[25]

Rainer Maria Rilke was evidently probing this collapse when, right at the beginning of the first of the *Duino Elegies*—a priority in itself suggestive—he intimated that the most sensitive ("the shrewd") are already awake to the decatenation of our modern world: "Die findigen Tiere merken es schon dass wir nicht sehr verlässlich zu Haus sind in der gedeuteten Welt."[26] 'Interpreted' in this context seems to have the force of 'interpreted in the way that *we* do', with the implication that it is *mis*interpreted. He then goes on to enumerate the few simple things—a tree, a slope, a walk— that still possess a personal significance for us in a world that, as *now* interpreted, gives us little sense of being at home, of Being-at-home. Things, he appears to be saying, have become what Heidegger styled "present-at-hand" rather than "ready-to-hand"; they have become mere objects scattered about and not related to us in any important way and without relation to each other. Things have been to a considerable degree stripped of their humanized, domesticated quality. Rilke, who spoke at an early stage of feeling that he was "more and more becoming the disciple of things,"[27] much later wrote of

the ever swifter vanishing of so much that is visible, whose place will not be supplied. Even for our grandparents a "House," a "Well," a familiar tower, their very dress, their cloak, was infinitely more, infinitely more intimate: almost everything a vessel in which they found and stored humanity. Now there came crowding over from America empty, indifferent things, pseudo-things, *dummy-life* . . . A house, in the American understanding, an American apple or vine, has *nothing* in common with the house, the fruit, the grape into which the hope and meditation of our forefathers had entered. The animated, experienced things *that share our lives* are coming to an end and cannot be replaced.[28]

Rilke and Nietzsche were among the first to point to this wornoutness of things and of the words attached to them, but the process has accelerated enormously since their time. Even on the simplest day-to-day level this degradation of things is remarkable. On the one hand, the sheer *number* of things has depreciated any particular one of them; on the other, our reckless destruction of things has sundered us from them in spirit. Things as beautiful in form and as brilliant in graphic presentation as our aluminum and cardboard containers, things as mechanically marvelous as our automobiles, things as eloquent as our old buildings, are coldly thrown aside, crushed, or torn down long before the expiration of their usefulness, and without regard for the genius that went into their production or the human involvement in their use. Our problem is now seen to lie not so much in how to create as in how to destroy things, in how to deal with our 'waste' so as to make place for the constant torrent of new and 'better' things. But though they are shiny, smell new, or are novel, things are no longer precious (however expensive they may be), and since we are not over against things but, as Rilke says, "share our lives" with them, the preciousness of our lives and of others' is diminished. We no longer mend or patch up or replace a part: we throw out and buy anew, bigger and more than before. Everything is disposable; we live in a Kleenex culture![29]

The theme is one that Heidegger took up. He was concerned especially that 'being' should have become as it seemed to him no more than an empty word, but he added that many words, and precisely the essential ones, were in the same situation. He was at pains to emphasize that the reason for the emptiness of the word 'being' lay in "the destroyed relation to Being as such."[30] He himself did not carry this over into the realm of existents, but it seems quite logical, and indeed necessary, to make this extension. If the words and things of a culture are emptied out and become mere appelatives—terminal moraines, as it were, from a vanished glacier—then the culture must already have fallen apart at the seams. And as meaning continues to be eliminated from the world and from man (meaning in the sense of an answer to Heidegger's question, "Why are there essents, why is there anything at all, rather than nothing?")[31] it seems inevitable that boredom and hyperboredom will become increasingly powerful forces in Western culture. Heidegger himself pointed to the question as being "upon us in boredom, when we are equally removed from despair and joy, and everything about us seems so hopelessly commonplace[32] that we no longer care whether anything is, or is not," going on to say that "with this the question . . . is evoked in a particular form."[33] But he does not appear to perceive that it is the half-conscious awareness that there *is* no satisfactory answer to the question that gives rise to the boredom. "How does it stand with Being?" asks Heidegger, and he answers that "Being has become little more than a mere word and its meaning an evanescent vapour."[34] If we substitute for 'Being' the phrase 'that which is experienced as of fundamental significance', what Auden in one of his poems refers to as 'Law', then it seems the merest truism that "Law is no more/ Law has gone away."[35]

What Rilke and Heidegger and many others all seem to be pointing to in their own ways is the process first of dedivinizing man, then of dehumanizing things, and finally of derealizing things.[36] Each is giving his commentary on the final stages along the road from Plato and Aristotle: the way of Western dualism descending through the nominalism of Ockham, the *esprit géometrique* of Descartes, the positivism of Comte and latter-day scientism—the "barbarism of reflection" that Vico pointed to in the early eighteenth century[37]—the dichotomy that has succeeded, to cite Auden again, in "parting/All that we feel from all that we perceive,/Desire from Data."[38]

With the removal, or gradual erosion, of a center, there has come into being a vacuum, and this has given rise both to anxiety and to boredom, two states that are in reality allotropes.[39] They are both spiritual equivalents of the agoraphobia, the *horror vacui*, the response to what Sartre calls the "monstrous spontaneity" of consciousness, the "vertigo of possibility" at which consciousness,

noting what could be called the fatality of its spontaneity, is suddenly anguished: it is this dread, absolute and without remedy, this fear of itself, which seems to be constitutive of pure consciousness, . . . If the *I* of *I Think* is the primary structure of consciousness, this dread is impossible.[40]

But the ego, which in normal times when the ideological structure of society is unshaken, effectively masks this spontaneity, in a period when all values and world views are radically called into doubt, is far less able to prevent the absolute from breaking through. The ego is not—as is consciousness—constituted separately from and independent of society; it is the *Da* of *Dasein,* and as such is implicated in the state of society and of its culture. Provided the individual can remain fixated on things and on the self, then what Heidegger calls "what-is-in-totality" is kept at bay. But let one's hold on these relax or falter, and

this wholeness overcomes us—for example in real boredom. . . . This profound boredom, drifting hither and thither in the abysses of existence like a mute fog, draws all things, all men and oneself along with them, reveals what-is-in-totality.[41]

The latter compound noun is Heidegger's way of referring to the essential existential situation, or in a word, reality. Though he goes on to speak particularly of 'dread', the "for example" in the foregoing quotation and the overall sense of what he says makes his remarks about this mood equally applicable to boredom: "All things, and we with them, sink into a kind of indifference . . . There is nothing to hold onto."[42] And there is "nothing to hold onto" because things have become—merely things, *praeterea nihil.* Beings have become sundered from Being, the Great Chain of Being has been reduced to a heap of links unattached to one another and unattached to anything at all other than themselves.

It has become a matter of grasping the individual thing in its utter individuality and disjunction, a final—possibly despairing—nominalism à outrance, culminating in, for example, the novels of Robbe-Grillet, which almost totally limit themselves to meticulous physical description, or in the work of various schools of contemporary art, in which the attempt is made to isolate and nail down *some* physical existence, however thin, meager, or minimal. Susan Sontag makes somewhat the same point in suggesting that we "contrast the benign nominalism proposed by Rilke . . . with the brutal nominalism adopted by many other artists."[43] It is her view that

the attachment of contemporary art to the "minimal" narrative principle of the catalogue or inventory seems almost to parody the capitalist world view, in which the environment is atomized into "items" (a category embracing things and persons, works of art, and natural organisms), in which every item is a commodity [in] a general leveling of value.[44]

However, there seems to be no reason to confine this 'atomization' and 'leveling' to any one political and economic system. The signs are that the same forces are operative in the Soviet-dominated sphere, though so far largely repressed, manipulated, or decelerated by the state apparatus. Easterners no less than Westerners are the heirs to the "barbarism of reflection," subject to "the dominant trait of Soviet life that Zbigniew Brzezinski has so aptly called the 'bureaucratization of boredom'."[45]

NOTES

1. Johann Wolfgang von Goethe, *Faust,* trans. Louis MacNeice (New York: Oxford University Press, 1960), p. 48, Faust's Study.

2. Otto Fenichel, "Zur Psychologie der Langweile," *Imago* 20 (1934):270.

3. Ernest G. Schachtel, *Metamorphosis* (New York: Basic Books, 1959), p. 234.

4. Ibid., p. 177. Cf. Kierkegaard's reference to "the *daemonic* spirit of boredom" (*Either/ Or* [Princeton, N.J.: Princeton University Press, 1944], p. 287).

5. Schachtel, *Metamorphosis,* p. 232.

6. Edward Bibring, "The Mechanism of Depression," in *Affective Disorders,* ed. Phyllis Greenacre (New York: International Universities Press, 1953), p. 32–33.

7. *The Message in the Bottle* (New York: Farrar, Straus & Giroux, 1975), p. 87.

8. Max Scheler, *Ressentiment* (New York: Free Press, 1961), pp. 70–71. The connection between "general negativism" and generalized boredom is very striking.

9. John Dewey, *Experience and Education* (New York: Macmillan, 1938), p. 44.

10. Ibid.

11. C. Wright Mills, *Power, Politics and People* (London: Oxford University Press, 1963), p. 331.

12. R. D. Laing, *The Politics of Experience* (New York: Random House, Ballantine Books, 1967), pp. 27–28.

13. Ibid., pp. 118–19.

14. Lewis Mumford, *The Pentagon of Power* (New York: Harcourt Brace Jovanovich, 1964), p. 368.

15. Kenneth Burke, *Permanence and Charge: An Anatomy of Purpose* (Los Altos, Calif.: Hermes Publications, 1954), p. 10.

16. Alan Watts, *The Wisdom of Insecurity* (New York: Random House, Vintage Books, 1951), pp. 114–15. Pascal, of course, went much further: "Men are so necessarily mad, that not to be mad would be to give a mad twist to madness" (Blaise Pascal, *Pensées* [Baltimore: Penguin Books, 1966], p. 148).

17. Nietzsche's playful suggestion was that "wherever a deep discontent with existence becomes prevalent, it is the after effects of some great dietary mistake made by a whole

people over a long period of time that are coming to light" (*The Gay Science* [New York: Random House, Vintage Books, 1974], p. 186). He suggests alcohol poisoning in the case of Europe! There is no lack of more recent candidates, sugar in particular.

18. John Macquarrie, *Martin Heidegger* (Richmond, Va.: John Knox Press, 1968), p. 20.

19. William Barrett, *Irrational Man* (New York: Doubleday & Co., 1962), p. 221.

20. Martin Heidegger, *Being and Time*, trans. J. Macquarrie and E. S. Robinson (London: SCM, 1962), p. 176 (emphasis added).

21. Ibid., p. 29.

22. Ibid., p. 167.

23. Anton Chekhov, *Six Plays*, ed. Robert W. Corrigan (New York: Holt, Rinehart & Winston, 1962), *Three Sisters*, p. 229. As Vershinin later remarks, "there's a great void which can't be filled. Humanity is passionately searching for something to fill that void, and, of course, it will find something someday" (p. 284).

24. "Every *Weltanschauung* is a conspiracy . . . we . . . have been trapped into sanity in our childhood" (Peter L. Berger, *Invitation to Sociology* [Harmondsworth, Eng.: Penguin, 1963], pp. 78, 82).

25. Martin Heidegger, *An Introduction to Metaphysics* (Garden City, N.Y.: Doubleday & Co., Anchor Books, 1961), pp. 37–41.

26. Rainer Maria Rilke, *Duino Elegies* (New York: W. W. Norton & Co., 1963), p. 21: "Already the shrewd beasts are aware that we don't feel very securely at home in our interpreted world" (my translation).

27. Erich Heller, *The Disinherited Mind* (Cleveland: World Publishing Co., 1959), p. 142.

28. Extract from Rilke's letter of 13 November 1925 to his Polish translator, *Duino Elegies*, p. 129.

29. "Cut off from every root, we have achieved the feat of breaking not only with the depths of things, but with their very surface" (E. M. Cioran, *The Fall into Time* [Chicago: Quadrangle, 1970], p. 67). What Cioran does not point out is that the surface *depends upon* the depths, and that the observable disintegration gives witness to a more fundamental process of dissolution.

30. Heidegger, *Introduction to Metaphysics*, p. 42.

31. Ibid., pp. 1–2.

32. Marcel referred to his own experience of this loss as "interior indigence . . . the feeling of an absence or rather of a non-presence. The ground ceases to echo beneath my feet. The world becomes thin and transparent. There is no more resistance, no more elasticity. I do not even set up resistance to myself, I no longer expect anything, either from myself or from events. Boredom, bound up, if I am not putting it too boldly, with a kind of pejorative awareness of intelligibility, of the 'of course'" (*Metaphysical Journal* [London: Rockliff, 1952], p. 302).

33. Heidegger, *Introduction to Metaphysics*, p. 2.

34. Ibid., p. 41. Cf. Schachtel, who cites Grassi's observation that "in the suffocation of boredom man experiences, on the one hand, nothingness, or non-being, and—in the *unbearable* quality of boredom—being" (*Metamorphosis*, p. 177 n. 9).

35. W. H. Auden, *The Collected Poetry* (New York: Random House, 1945), p. 75.

36. Another harbinger of this dissolution of meaning was Hugo von Hoffmansthal, speaking through the experiences of Roquentin, the writer of the *Briefe eines Zürückkehrten*. Rational terms and arguments become invalid, ideas and ideologies lose their reality. Only individual objects, discrete facts, remain: "Objects are just what they appear to be: behind them there is nothing." Eventually even the single object dissolves into "une pâte même des choses," as Sartre writes in *La nausée* (Heller, *Disinherited Mind*, p. 178). Cf. Georges

Bernanos: "The boredom of man overcomes everything, vicar, it will bring about the deliquescence of the world" (*Oeuvres romanesques* [Paris: Gallimard, Bibliothèque de la Pléiade, 1961], p. 1464).

37. *The New Science of Giambattista Vico*, trans. T. G. Bergin and M. H. Fisch (Ithaca, N.Y.: Cornell University Press, 1970), p. 1.

38. Auden, *Collected Poetry*, p. 341.

39. There is a level at which there ceases to be any significant difference between the two, both arising out of a sense of the void, "Past and pure Naught, complete monotony." It is of this level that Hans Jonas writes that "Gnostic man is thrown into an antagonistic, anti-divine, and therefore anti-human nature, modern man into an indifferent one. Only the latter represents the absolute vacuum, the really bottomless pit. . . . From that nature no direction at all can be elicited. That nature does not care one way or the other, is the true abyss. That only man cares, in his finitude facing nothing but death, alone with his contingency and the *objective meaninglessness* of his projected meanings, is *a truly unprecedented situation*" (*The Gnostic Religion* [Boston: Beacon Press, 1963], p. 339, emphasis added).

40. Jean-Paul Sartre, *The Transcendence of the Ego* (New York: Farrar, Straus & Giroux, Noonday Press, 1957), p. 102.

41. Martin Heidegger, "What Is Metaphysics?" in *Existence and Being*, ed. W. Brock (Chicago: Henry Regnery Co., 1949), p. 364.

42. Ibid., p. 366.

43. Susan Sontag. "The Aesthetics of Silence," in *The Discontinuous Universe*, edd.

44. Ibid., p. 68.

45. Peter L. Berger, "The Socialist Myth," *The Public Interest* 44 (1976), p. 11.

4 • The Collapse of Common Sense

There, through the broken branches go
The ravens of unresting thought.

W. B. Yeats

In this web of belief every strand depends upon every other
strand, and a Zande cannot get out of its meshes because it is
the only world he knows. The web is not an external structure
in which he is enclosed. It is the texture of his thought and he
cannot think that his thought is wrong.

E. Evans-Pritchard

I wonder whether the world is anchored anywhere, if she is she
swings with an uncommon long cable.

Herman Melville

The view that boredom is an original deposit in Man has been
found to be inadequate; it has been established that only in some
instances can boredom be at all attributed to the mechanism of
repression. The task of explaining its position in recent Western
culture and its remarkable growth in and since the eighteenth
century is now that of answering the question, What specific historical developments have occurred that have tilted the balance in
Western man toward boredom?

It is of course boredom,—hyperboredom—that is in question.
The problem, that is to say, is not merely that people at a particular
time lack a sense of purpose and drift around in a state of psychic
doldrums waiting for a wind to come up to give them propulsion
toward a destination that they themselves cannot identify, but that,
as time will show, nonetheless exists. In hyperboredom, the question is not accidental, capable of solution by a deus ex machina, but
is at the heart of the matter, and it raises the whole question of the
point of human existence. Possible destinations and objectives
abound, but that very fact seems to cast doubt on the primacy of
any, and even on the validity of all, giving rise to what Karl Mannheim called "the crisis in valuation," arising from the "chaos of

74

competing and unreconciled valuations."[1] But this crisis, which Nietzsche perceived a good half-century before Mannheim wrote of it in the 1940s,[2] is itself only the acute stage of a slow process of erosion going back into the heart of the Middle Ages. The so-called medieval synthesis, the integration of the whole range of Greek thought (and not just neo-Platonism) into the structure of Christian theology, the welcoming of dialectic and the logical categories of Greek rationalism, the sum of which has so often been represented as the establishment of an integrated foundation for European thought—were all in reality the continuation of a process of cultural unraveling that came to a temporary halt during the long period that saw the dissolution of the Roman Empire and the gradual emergence of the medieval kingdoms, the Holy Roman Empire, and the papacy. This period saw the emergence of Christian culture on a largely non-Aristotelian, neo-Platonic basis. In the wake of Aristotle's reception into western European philosophy in the eleventh and twelfth centuries, Saint Bernard of Clairvaux, the harsh and determined adversary of Peter Abelard's teaching at the University of Paris, perceived one tendency within the process of rational questioning—the method of Abelard's *Sic et Non*—and foresaw its to him *certain* effect on the fabric of faith, and he acted accordingly. He would no doubt have assailed Saint Thomas Aquinas on the same grounds, as in fact did latter-day Bernards who, however, lacked his vehement skill and who, moreover, lived in the age of the full flood of Aristotle's works. It is now possible to see that these works had the effect of a Trojan Horse,[3] but it was not until the following century, above all in the works of William of Ockham and the nominalists, that, to cite Copleston,

> the wedge was driven between theology and philosophy . . . through their critical analysis of the metaphysical ideas and arguments of their predecessors the nominalists *left faith hanging in the air without (so far as philosophy is concerned) any rational basis.*[4]

In Saint Thomas it is still *fides quaerens intellectum,* the intellect driving on as far as possible to grasp the meaning of faith, which in any apparent clash between the two, unquestionably prevails. But with Ockham,

> theology and philosophy tend to fall apart . . . philosophy tends to take on more and more a 'lay' character . . . Truths which he believed but which he did not think could be philosophically

proved he relegated to the sphere of faith. . . . This would imply the possibility of *two* ethics.[5]

Instead of analysis and critical discussion of the application of accepted metaphysical principles, this was an assault on the metaphysical principles themselves. Ockham's work has since then become recognizable as a major stage in that secularization of thought, that breach between faith and reason (reason at least in the sense of 'rationality', and the very distinction itself marks a crucial shift in thinking), which over the course of the succeeding six centuries has sunk into the deepest fibers of Western culture and which has penetrated into the world view not merely of a handful of scholastics or intellectuals, but of the man in the street and the child sitting in front of the television set.[6] In Ockham's time, and for long after, the 'truths' of theology prevailed almost effortlessly over what might appear to be the contrary 'truths' of philosophy, but a crack had, for all that, begun to open up between the two that no number of papal bulls would ultimately be able to paper over.

Since this earliest and smallest beginning, one after another of the unthought certitudes of Western man have been brought into the light of day, for all the world like denizens of the lower depths of the oceans fished up to the surface, exploding as they emerge. The destructive exposure of each deep belief has been another blow to the fabric of reality, to that social structure of certainty which we call common sense, the self-evident *Weltanschauung* that is perhaps the most essential cement in any culture, since it is the source of meaning, creation, and control.[7]

While every society has its 'common sense', what constitutes common sense is by no means common to all societies—though each may suppose that it is or at any rate should be—so that the phrase really means "what our group holds to be the case." But it is rarely seen as meaning that and nothing more. Those referring to it in their own culture assume that it signifies what actually *is* the case, and it may take a protracted barrage of powerful and varied shocks to bring about a shift of perception in relation to even one element of what one might call the 'of-course world' of an entire society. And such a barrage is just what Western culture has undergone since the premonitory tremors of the fourteenth century. The effect of the Babylonian Captivity, of the Reformation, of the Thirty Years' War, of the dual political revolutions in England, of the Copernican revolution, and of the voyages of discovery, to mention only some of the most shattering developments in the three centuries following Ockham, constitutes in the philosophical and psychological aggregate what Thomas Kuhn called, in relation to scientific theory, "paradigm rejection," or more simply, the collapse of common sense.[8]

The extent of the collapse even as early as the first half of the seventeenth century appears particularly clearly in the writings of Blaise Pascal, and it will not, of course, escape notice that he was also the first 'modern' writer to expatiate on boredom. "One meridian," he wryly observes, "determines what is true," and "law has its periods." He then goes on to demolish the conventional wisdom, the notion of 'law' written into the fabric of being:

> They allege that justice does not lie in these customs, but resides in natural laws common to every country. They would certainly maintain this obstinately if the reckless chance which distributed human laws had struck on just one which was universal, but the joke is that man's whims have shown such great variety that there is not one.[9]

He sees the problem quite acutely, and with astonishingly modern clarity, although to him it is not yet an insoluble problem because he can still hold on to truth by revelation, truth even in spite of a contrary finding by reason, a sort of seventeenth-century version of Tertullian's *credo quia absurdum* ("I believe precisely *because* it is absurd").

> Merely according to reason, nothing is just in itself, everything shifts with time. Custom is the whole of equity for the sole reason that it is accepted. That is the mystic basis of its authority. Anyone who tries to bring it back to its first principle destroys it.[10]

And he is even aware of the fatal effect of letting the cat out of the bag:

> Men must often be deceived for their own good . . . The truth about the usurpation of the law must not be made apparent; it came about originally without reason and has become reasonable. We must see that it is regarded as authentic and eternal, and its origins must be hidden if we do not want it soon to end.[12]

A modern expression of the belief that those in the know must keep their knowledge from the rest occurs in the work of Vilfredo Pareto. As Raymond Aron paraphrases his thought,

> one cannot explain by the logico-experimental method what the social order actually is without destroying its foundation. Society is held together only by feelings, which are not true, but which are effective. If the sociologist shows people the wrong side of the embroidery or what goes on behind the scenes, he runs the risk of destroying indispensable illusions.[12]

One can see the natural-law paradigm and its theological underpinning, Christianity, coming apart at the seams. Shakespeare, of course, had Hamlet put it much more succinctly to the ultimate paradigmatics, Rosencrantz and Guildenstern: "There is nothing good or bad, but thinking makes it so." Although it is never safe to attribute to the playwright the sentiments of any of his characters, a character could not have had the thought unless his creator had it first, and even the thinking of the thought indicates a critical shift.

The essential nature of the shift has most recently and most fully been analyzed by Michel Foucault, and he refers to it as "an enormous reorganization of culture"[12] that occurred in the sixteenth century—the ousting of the hermeneutic view of the world by the semiological. Man gradually ceased to believe in the project of tracing out *the* order of things, through "digging out the ancient Word from the unknown places where it may be hidden,"[14] and came to pursue the task of making *an* order of things. The sign/ word came to be seen as that which happens to be attached to the thing; there is no internal, necessary (though ciphered) connection arising out of the common origin of both, that is, God. As John Keble put it very simply two centuries ago: "There is a book, who runs may read, / Which heavenly truth imparts." The "book" is that of Creation, whose contents in earlier centuries were seen as similitudes, as indicators of an Absolute Signified; the world was apprehended as "one vast, single text."[15] Everything was as itself a sign, nature being

> trapped in the thin layer that holds semiology and hermeneutics one above the other . . . The truth of all these marks—whether they are woven into nature itself or whether they exist in lines on parchments and in libraries—is everywhere the same: coeval with the institution of God.[16]

Language was "a thing inscribed in the fabric of the world,"[17] so

that Shakespeare was voicing the actual, general view of his age—
not just expressing a poetic or fanciful thought—when he wrote of
"tongues in trees, books in the running brooks, / Sermons in stones,
and good in everything."[18]

"Good in everything," because nothing that signified God could
be anything else, and everything *did* signify God. Properly interpreted, all things pointed upward convergently toward the Absolute Signified; everything was, quite simply, significant, including
falling sparrows and the number of hairs on a man's head. Above all
was Man, "God's privileged signifier"[19] made, in the words of the
catechism, "in the image and likeness of God" and therefore de-
pendent for his meaning, and for the meaning of the world, upon
God. "God's in His heaven—/ All's right with the world." In such a
cosmos nothing could be profoundly boring, in Heidegger's sense,
in the sense of hyperboredom, for the importance of everything
was guaranteed, even if God's ways might not be our ways. Everything was important—if not evidently and at the time, then *sub
specie aeternitatis.*

But Shakespeare also clearly had a sense of a transition, and
though he seems to be expressing the thought of dissolution only as
a possibility, even this sense of possibility was new:

> The heavens themselves, the planets, and this centre
> Observe degree, priority, and place,
> Insisture, course, proportion, season, form,
> Office, and custom, in all line of order.
> . . . O! When degree is shak'd
> Which is the ladder to all high designs,
> The enterprise is sick! . . .
> Take but degree away, untune that string,
> And, hark, what discord follows! each thing meets
> In mere oppugnancy.[20]

At a time when, at least so far as the written record goes, others
were absorbed in debate about which branch of what all agreed to
be the true faith was the truest, Shakespeare almost alone—if not
entirely so—seems to have entertained the thought that *all* belief
might be equally misguided. Later in *Troilus and Cressida* he puts
the key question into Troilus's mouth: "What is aught, but as 'tis
valued?"[21] Kaufman says of Shakespeare's work that it "stands as a
monument of a tradition that is frequently forgotten today, and it
celebrates the riches of a world without God,"[22] but what he
strangely omits to mention is that the reason for this lack of atten-

tion lies in the fact that Shakespeare had few, if any, concelebrants. It is true that Donne, in "The Progresse of the Soule," written some years later, might seem to be echoing Troilus's radical doubt when he declares:

> There's nothing simply good, nor ill alone,
> Of every quality comparison
> The only measure is, and judge, opinion.[23]

Further evidence for this impression could be perceived in lines from a later work: "And new Philosophy calls all in doubt . . . / 'Tis all in peeces, all cohaerence gone; / All just supply and all Relation.[24] But though he was a skeptic, he was no atheist, as his subsequent career as dean of Saint Paul's and the strong faith of his sermons in that capacity attest.[25] The "new Philosophy" (the geocentric model of the universe first proposed by Copernicus and worked out by Kepler and Galileo) came into a context that prevented it from seriously disturbing the faith of even such a probing mind as Donne's. Nonetheless, these lines and numerous others are significant as indicating the powerful disturbance the revolution in astronomy caused in a still overwhelmingly religious society and justify Nietzsche's remark two and a half centuries later that "since Copernicus man has been rolling from the center toward X,"[26] for Copernicus and his congeners gave a catastrophic jolt to what William James called "the sentiment of rationality." That "ceremony of innocence"[27] whose drowning Yeats mourned in the twentieth century, that same "goddess ceremony, with a crown of all the stars" which the poet celebrated in the seventeenth, is the very same "custom" that James pointed to as the "source of whatever rationality the thing may gain in our thought."

The crucial but only very gradually realized effect of the new cosmic scheme was to remove 'degree'—that is, a divinely instituted and from a human point of view *arbitrary* order—and to substitute a law intelligible in human terms and comprehensible within a humanly devised mathematical plan, but ultimately without any necessary meaning for man, and by the same token to make man a mere item in the vast cosmic inventory. The plan is an exclusively quantitative one. As E. A. Burtt wrote, "For Kepler . . . the real world is a world of quantitative characteristics only; its differences are differences of number alone." He goes on to cite Kepler himself and his declaration that "wherever there are qualities, there are likewise quantities, but not always vice versa."[28]

James did not get right to the heart of the matter in suggesting that there is an equivalence between custom and theoretic insight: "The daily contemplation of phenomena juxtaposed in a certain order begets an acceptance of their connection as absolute as the repose engendered by theoretic insight into their coherence,"[29] for it is not the vertical coherence *among* that is vital, but the horizontal coherence *with*, with a center, that maintains the evidently culturally necessary sentiment of *meaningfulness.* If theoretic insight did in fact lead to repose, we should (at least until the work of Heisenberg and Bohr) have been becoming more reposeful rather than, as was evidently the case, less. James was alive to the human need for coherence and maintained that "if the each-form [the pluralist rather than the monist 'all-form'] be the eternal form of reality no less than it is the form of temporal appearance, we still have a coherent world."[30]

But the question is, *Who* is included in the 'we'? Are more than a few able to accept a world in which there is horizontal but not vertical coherence? What if, though everything forms a "universal co-implication, or integration of all things *durcheinander,*"[31] they do not together refer to something other than themselves, to something from which they *all* derive their being? It would have been more consistent with James's general approach—and to subsequent reality—if he had held to what he had written in the preceding chapter:

> I saw that . . . an *intellectual* answer to the intellectualists' difficulties will never come, and that the real way out of them, far from consisting in the discovery of such an answer, consists in simply closing one's ears to the question.[32]

Intellectualism seems in fact to have become self-defeating, for it has done much to produce a dehumanized world, a world so distasteful to man that he has turned his back either on it or on the intellectual process itself. No one put this better than James himself: "A nameless *unheimlichkeit* comes over us at the thought of there being nothing eternal in our final purposes."[33]

Now, in the natural sciences, once one paradigm has come to be perceived as making better sense of the phenomena than another, it entirely, rapidly, and without appeal ousts its predecessor. Outside the empirical field, however, old paradigms can survive long after new ones have been formulated, so that it is quite possible that no more than a few people can see that a change is called for.

Monarchy, for example, persisted long after its paradigmatic rationale, the divine right of kings, had been rejected—in England in 1688, elsewhere at other times. As in science, it might seem that it was merely a matter of quantitative change: Charles I beheaded, James II forced into exile, William of Orange invited to take over the vacant throne—each breach of the 'rule' specially justified to save the appearances. But as Thomas Kuhn points out in relation to another departed theory, "the proliferation of versions of a theory is a very usual sympton of crisis."[34]

"Proliferation of versions" exactly describes what has taken place since the fourteenth century: the gradual dissolution of the post-Socratic, essentially Aristotelian paradigm of reason has over-lapped the much more defined and unequivocal dismantling of Aristotelian cosmology, physics, and natural science in general. It is an incidental irony that Saint Thomas Aquinas succeeded in grafting Aristotle onto Christianity with such thoroughness that, as the whole structure of Greek thought has come more and more under fire, Christianity itself has suffered for its alliance with what is essentially pagan thought, unnecessary for, and even in some respects contrary to, the heart of the Christian message.

The crumbling of the citadel of Greek rationalism is obscured by the distractions afforded by the detailed alterations to Western man's view of himself and of the world. Columbus did not so much discover a new world as *de*-discover the old Aristotelian-Ptolemaic one. The crucial significance of his voyage—and even more of Magellan's—was not that it brought more information about the hitherto unknown world, but that it helped to undermine the notion that the general structure of truth was known. Copernicus's rearrangement of the universe was a no less destructive blow to the idea that truth was known in essence, even if not yet completely. It added to that feeling fatal to common sense that truth is open-ended. From these, and numerous relatively lesser intellectual turnabouts (such as Harvey's discovery of the circulation of the blood), must have come much of the distrust of reason that went so deep in Pascal. If men could be so greatly deceived for so long in matters so fundamental, then surely any structure man might build could have been erected on equally flawed foundations. A *feeling* of truth might mean nothing, as an impression of seeing might be no more than the effect of a mirage, and yet, "the heart has its reasons of which reason knows nothing."[35]

What was being driven out was the ability to rest on any authority, whether Aristotle, Saint Thomas, the Scriptures or the

Fathers, so that Descartes wrote that his first rule "was to accept nothing as true which *I* did not clearly recognize to be so; to accept nothing more than was presented to my mind so clearly and distinctly that *I* could have no occasion to doubt it."[36] Descartes was a pioneer in seeking to establish truth on a systematic, purely rational basis, starting from absolute doubt and relying on nothing but his own powers of deduction, and his ground for doing so was his observation about philosophy that "it has been studied for many centuries by the most outstanding minds without having produced anything which is not in dispute and consequently doubtful." He also considered that he had to go about this fundamental task because he "felt that in all these ways we are much more greatly influenced by custom and example than by certain knowledge."[37]

It is quite possible to see in Descartes, Galileo, Pascal, and Newton potential atheists, or at least agnostics, who were prevented from seeing themselves as such because of the still all-pervasive Christian belief of the society they lived in (although the sharp-eyed Church did not overlook Galileo). This is to chime in with Bronowski and Mazlish's contention that Bayle, the compiler of the first of the Enlightenment encyclopaedias,

> demonstrated that, in spite of Descartes' religious affirmations, and in spite of Pascal's mysticism, the view which a sceptical enquiry was generally (and perhaps *ultimately*) bound to produce was Bayle's civilized and discreet agnosticism. [Emphasis added][38]

And here, in the rather unlikely person of a relatively minor author, can be seen very clearly evidence of the coming to consciousness of the paradigm rejection stemming from the breakdown of the medieval synthesis. In the new paradigm, which was then still forming, faith is no longer seeking reason; reason has ousted faith and is now bent upon detailing the mathematical and logical structure of the universe, a mechanism of exquisite, but natural, geometry.[39] Man is still distinct; but apart from his mind and his immortal soul, he is like other animals, also a machine, a troublesome dualism to be sure, which has only fully surfaced since the latter part of the nineteenth century to become acute in our own time. To cite Kuhn again, "Today research in parts of philosophy, psychology and linguistics, and even art history, all converge to suggest that the traditional paradigm is somehow askew."[40] But the true "traditional paradigm," traditional not only for this culture, but for virtually *all* cultures, was radically undermined in the West centuries ago. What Kuhn is referring to is simply a shift *within* the scientific paradigm, as, say, conversion to Christianity from Judaism, or from Christianity to Islam would represent a shift within the traditional one. The "askew"-ness of the traditional paradigm is actually the second and final stage in the eradication of its Western form, the medieval world view. In the first stage, empirical investigation rapidly supplanted theology as the mode of explanation *within* the physical world; in the second, it has become the universal and exclusive epistemological principle.[41] Now the residual dualism of mind and matter, of teleology and mechanism, of choice and determination, is being resolved by the reduction of mind to 'mind' (the final elimination of the Ghost in the Machine), in the reduction of reason to rationalization, and in the reduction of action to reaction (the product of conditioning or of genetic or social programming).

The nature of this crucial shift has been expressed in a number of ways. Schiller, in a phrase Weber later picked up, referred to it as "die Entzäuberung der Welt." Mircea Eliade, a century and a half later, spoke of it as "the desacralization of the cosmos," seeing it as "accomplished by scientific thought" and as "an integral part of the gigantic transformation of the world undertaken by the industrial societies."[42] To Karl Jaspers, the process was that of the "de-spiritualization of the world."[43] Nietzsche described the situation he perceived in a number of ways, all under the general rubric of 'nihilism', and wrote of "the end of the *moral* interpretation of the world which no longer has any sanctions,"[44] later expressly tying this in to religion:

> The time has come when we have to pay for having been Christians for two thousand years: we are losing the *center of gravity* by virtue of which we lived.[45] . . . The entire idealism of mankind hitherto is on the point of changing suddenly into nihilism, i.e., meaninglessness. [Emphasis added][46]

Common to all these formulations is a perception that a previously unspoken, largely unreflective fund of meaning has been dissipated; that natural authority, the air-breathed 'common sense' of our society, has become rarefied almost to exhaustion, and, as Robert Nisbet pointed out some years ago, "boredom is one of the most dangerous accompaniments of the loss of authority in a social order . . . boredom born of natural authority dissolved, of too long exposure to the void."[47] In light of this penetrating comment it might seem strange that he should have then fallen back on the commonplace attribution of boredom to "the sense of goals accomplished, of affluence possessed," and should have dwelt, in a more recent work, on the contribution of increased leisure. However, the idea that leisure leads ot boredom is one that can be traced back at least two millennia; to Horace, for example, urging the need for manual labor to combat its effects; to Seneca, writing of leisure as a "vice," and warning one of his correspondents that "it must be shaken off by occupation"; to similar warnings in Old and New Testaments, from the Book of Ecclesiasticus to the letters of Saint Paul. Among more recent writers, Ernest Schachtel considers that

> boredom is the malaise of our civilization, with its relatively large amount of leisure time, and that this sickness is manifested both in the wide spread of acute boredom and in the frantic activities to escape boredom.[49]

As against this, an entirely opposite idea of leisure—that it is the true condition of man—is at least as ancient, going back to Aristotle, for whom "we are unleisurely [*a-skolia*] in order that we may have leisure [*skole*]."[50] As a modern proponent of this view maintains,

> leisure is possible only on the premise that man consents to his own true nature, and abides in concord with the meaning of the universe (whereas idleness . . . is the refusal of such consent). Leisure draws its vitality from affirmation. It is not the same as non-activity . . . The provision of an external opportunity for leisure is not enough; it can only be fruitful if the man himself is capable of leisure and can, as we say, "occupy his leisure," or (as the Greeks still more clearly say), *skolen agein*, "work his leisure" (this usage brings out the by no means "leisurely" character of leisure).[51]

And what is meant by "work his leisure" is no mere filling of 'spare time' with pastimes, hobbies, and crafts to keep oneself 'occupied' (a telling word in its suggestion that we are somehow 'empty') or to make a 'change of pace', as if speed were the problem, irrespective of or rather than, destination. In this view, the person bored by 'leisure' (a state of not-working) is a person who is in actuality also bored by work but is too busy most of the time to realize it, and the fundamental reason for his being bored by work *and* by leisure is that there is something about his situation in the world that is not in accord with his true nature. He could echo Baudelaire in saying that "one must work, if not for taste then at least from despair. For, to reduce everything to a single truth: work is less boring than pleasure." Or put otherwise, not-working is less effective in blocking out boredom than working—a sentiment with which Pascal would have concurred before his sudden illumination.

Looked at in this perspective, it is possible to see that the Roman authors, Pascal, and such modern authors as Schachtel should be understood as speaking only for particular historical situations. If we were to step outside the confines of particular phases in Western civilization and look at its culture at other times, or escape its limitations altogether and examine quite different cultures including those that we patronizingly refer to as 'primitive' (but which have not, or had not until recently, suffered a "loss of authority in a social order") we would be reminded that it is perfectly possible for leisure and 'play' to be highly productive and richly satisfying, to provide for, and at the same time to arise out of, the deepest form of personal and social cohesion. There is in fact no necessary connection between leisure and boredom—or rather hyperboredom—and it is precisely in the failure to distinguish between these two fundamentally different states that there lies the explanation of the confused and oversimple explanations for its historical rise. As long as the word 'boredom' is regarded as pointing to one mental state (and a relatively unimportant one, notwithstanding the agonized and despairing cries of its victims), or more exactly, to one insignificant mental state with various superficial causes—rather on a par with some painful but not life-threatening allergy—its occurrence will continue to be misattributed to some fairly obvious social conditions or to some dark strain in man's nature.

It is of course tempting to link the growth of boredom to the achievement of power and possessions, as Lewis Mumford does:

> Nothing is more striking throughout history than the chronic disaffection, the malaise, the anxiety, and the psychotic self-destructiveness of the ruling classes, once they are in command of "all that the heart can desire." For the dominant minority, the privileged few, have always been faced with the ultimate curse of such a meaningless existence: sheer boredom.[52]

However, dominant minorities have *not* invariably, or even commonly, been subject to the experience of meaninglessness: dominance, in societies within the Common Human Pattern (see below, p. 100), brings no such collapse. It is only in cultures such as ours, from which the sense of transcendence is fading, or has already faded, that commanding "all that the heart can desire" tends to bring on "sheer boredom"—that is, hyperboredom. Though it is historically true that this kind of boredom was particularly rife among the privileged (that is to say, leisured) few from the eighteenth century onward, the relationship was not in fact a straightforward one of cause and effect. Several factors have made it difficult to discern this disjuncture and to perceive as the actual root of this novel boredom the growing metaphysical void at the center of Western civilization, not such more obvious conditions as wealth, leisure, personal pathology, or human nature. Until relatively recently, even the great majority of the privileged were protected against the effects and a full awareness of the situation by a certain inertial religiosity or piety, by ignorance, or by obtuseness. Time has now stripped these concealments from the rich, and as the poor have entered more fully into the culture they have come to share something of the same awareness and its effects. For them, dreams of wealth and ease became, with the growing chance of mobility in the later nineteenth century, an increasingly potent source of significance. The dreaming itself, the tense anticipatory excitement in the prospect of gratification, the satisfaction in the possibly slow move upward, the warming hope that at least one's children would enter the promised land—all served to conceal from them the departure of the gods. Now that the dreams have so largely been realized, it has become easier to see that they always had about them a symbolic quality, that they embodied desires so intense as to exceed any possible consummation, that they represented in actuality hopes for a paradise here and now (or some place soon) that had become unacknowledged surrogates for that paradise hereafter which had in considerable measure lost its grip upon the thinking of the mass of the people.

By a singular irony, the widespread achievement of hopes has thus not led to increased psychological or spiritual well-being but rather to a pervasive "anomie of affluence," as it has been called.[53] So many have achieved so much so fast that dreams of success have been overtaken by the reality and have lost their strength as sources of collective meaning binding society together. This is especially true of so many of the young, who come into a world of apparently almost infinite and easy plenty, but who experience it as in some indefinable way inadequate. They seem to be seeking, without even knowing what they are looking for, the missing center of gravity that would give weight to their existence, only to find, or to sense, that their culture provides none. It is not affluence and ease in themselves that have led to hyperboredom; they have merely let the sense of vacuity ensuing from the collapse of the "traditional paradigm" break through, just as in earlier times might going into the desert, into extreme physical and psychological deprivation.

Some comments Auden made on Dürer's etching, *Melencolia,* point to the factor that links the apparently polar opposites, satiety and deprivation, with hyperboredom. Seeking to explain why Dürer portrayed someone so richly endowed with creative possibilities as profoundly suffering, he suggested that the cause lay in the fact that

> surrounded by every possibility, she cannot find within herself or without *the necessity* to realize one rather than another. Urban society is, like the desert, a place without limits.

Of modern man he goes on to say that "he fails to find a necessity within himself" that will substitute for those hitherto supplied by tradition, mythology, and religion.[54]

Even given the latter, our tendency to psychic agoraphobia seems to make it essential for us to be enclosed within some frame of occupation, repetition, and even ritual. As far back as the fifth century in the Christian tradition (and much further in earlier religious forms), Saint Benedict of Nursia showed an intuitive grasp, in his *Holy Rule,* of the need, even among those of strong faith, to submit themselves to a discipline of mind and body if they were to be enabled to cleave to their purposes. The enemy was not so much possessions as vacancy, however poorly endowed, blank hours and days during which what Sartre the "disordered subjectivity," the "monstrous spontaneity," can break through and drive men 'out of their minds' into frenetic activity or bored indifference. The persisting error has been to equate this kind of vacancy—a temporary loss of momentum in a charted course—with the permanent stasis brought on by the absence or loss of all sense of meaning. As it happened, boredom from enforced inactivity and boredom from the diminishing effectiveness of religious faith came together in mutual reinforcement in the same area, France (more specifically, Versailles), during the same period of time, the latter part of the seventeenth and the whole of the eighteenth centuries. This coincidence, together with the existence of only a single term to refer to the two conditions, effectively masked, as it has continued to mask, their very different origins and significance. The more obvious and undeniable short-term cause, affluence (at least for the few), in conjunction with a rigidly indolent way of life, has kept the deep, long-term alteration in the European spirit from being perceived as, at the very least, the co-villain. In Madame du Deffand's perception of those around her as "des machines à ressort", one hears an echo of the results of the work of Descartes and Newton in creating a model of Man and the cosmos as essentially mechanical and void of divine or superhuman reference, except through making what may now be seen as a gratuitous and irrational addendum. The state this manner of thinking created is strongly reminiscent of Martin Marty's description of a variety of contemporary secularity:

> The majority . . . adhered to inherited religions; this majority, however, transformed them so significantly (if subtly) that one may speak of the change as one of controlled (ambiguous) secularity.[55]

But 'secularity'—another term to put alongside 'desacralization' and 'despiritualization'—leaves many, perhaps most, with no alternative but to *seek* a source of authority.

What is the connection between seeking authority—natural authority having dissolved, as Nisbet says—and boredom? Here again Nisbet gets close but fails to see the full implication of what he writes: "Youth is beyond question idealistic. But in our present society youth is so bored,"[56] for it is precisely because youth is 'idealistic' that it is bored,[57] much as the Israelites would have become bored with the golden calf they made themselves if Moses had not come down from cloud-covered Mount Sinai with the tablets of the Law, "written with the finger of God."[58] Idealism, if by that is meant the urgent desire to search out and to pursue what is excellent and what is true, to cultivate and to cleave to what is beautiful and right, becomes increasingly incapable of being satisfied, or even of finding a credible object or direction, in a culture where Truth has been reduced to truth, or even more damagingly to truths, or even to "truths."[59] This is the sense of Herman Hesse's comment in *Steppenwolf* that "there are times when a whole generation is caught between two ages, two modes of life, with the consequence that it loses all power to understand itself, and has no standard, no security, no simple acquiescence."[60] The limitation of this state of affairs merely to one generation is inadequate, but as a commentary on the trend *in the last six centuries,* the notion of the loss of "simple acquiescence" is extraordinarily apt and illuminating.

The whole idea of the modern world as in transition between two epochs can be found in numerous forms, associated with various gradations of boredom, from the most listless and hopeless to the hyperirritated, and Hegel, in giving voice to his perception of it, expressly connected it with boredom:

> The spirit of the time growing slowly and quietly ripe for the new form it is to assume, disintegrates one fragment after another of the structure of its previous world. Frivolity and again *ennui,* which are spreading in the established order of things, the undefined foreboding of something unknown, all these betoken that there is something else approaching.[61]

The former is perhaps best and most recently exemplified in the metaphor of expectation that runs through *Waiting for Godot,* in which a feeling of mankind's between-ness irradiates the entire play with a black light. Rilke gave poetic voice to an analogous, but more optimistic, sense of this situation in his Seventh Elegy: "Jede dumpfe Umkehr hat solche Enterbte/denen das Frühere nicht und noch nicht das Nächste gehört."[62] *Dumpf* can be variously translated as "dull," "hollow," or "gloomy," and its substantive, *Dumpfheit,* as "stupor" or "torpor," so that the meaning of the first line is that there are eras of transition that are stupefyingly dull because they are no longer alive with old purposes, and that there are some living in those ages, the Misfits,[63] who consciously reject the old, hollowed-out world, but for whom no new one yet exists. The thought has obvious echoes in the lines Eliot wrote a decade or two later: "We are the hollow men/We are the stuffed men/Leaning together/Headpieces filled with straw. Alas!"[64]

Foremost among the *enragés* was Nietzsche, who found the dreariness of the mediocre, shop-soiled, sleazy, utterly worn-out pieties of the nineteenth century intolerable. He, too, saw himself living between two ages: "'I come too early,' he said then; 'my time is not yet. This tremendous event . . . has not yet reached the ears of men.'"[65] The "tremendous event" was, of course, the death of God, God having in fact 'died of boredom,' stifled in the shard of man's stereotypes of Him—which is to say, rather, that Nietzsche saw his contemporaries as being in *their* spiritual death throes, boredom representing the symptoms of their psychic moribundity.[66] Much of his writing was an appeal against the deadness, the crushing tedium, the platitudes, the bourgeois religiosity of the pharisaism of his age, and in announcing that "nur wer sich wandelt, bleibt mit mir verwandt" (only he who *continues* to change is my blood brother),[67] he gave notice of the need to move on constantly from the dead, past, world—but to no particularly clearly indicated new one. To Schopenhauer, the need for change was no less paramount, but the escape lay inward, into nothingness, nirvana.

A century later Heidegger was writing, "We come too late for the gods, and too early for Being," while a cooler mid-century version of the selfsame theme comes in the work of C. Wright Mills: "The moral uneasiness of our time . . . is due to this key fact: the older values . . . no longer grip us, nor have they been replaced by new values and codes which would lend moral meaning."[68]

Now, if there is, as Nisbet says, "no standard" to stretch toward; if the older values "no longer grip us"; if there is no anchored ideal, just a progression; if "one grants the reality of becoming as the only reality, forbids oneself every kind of clandestine access to afterworlds and false divinities,"[69] then it is easy to understand why those most implicated in this normlessness—the young—should be so bored, for it seems that, constituted as we are, boredom is the inevitable accompaniment of the absence, or even serious uncertainty about the stability and reliability, of values, purposes, meanings and commitment.

And Hesse's perception, cited above, is absolutely accurate. Western culture moved first from a virtually universal acceptance of the Christian ethical ideals to an individualistic view such as that voiced by Schiller, for whom "every individual human being . . . bears within himself, as his potential and his destiny, the pure ideal of man. In this view, to be in accord with its immutable oneness through all changes is the great task of life."[70] But since his time, even that much external commitment has been dissipated, so that it now seems to vast numbers that, as Freud wrote, "the ego is not master in its own house."[71] With this has come the radical doubt of the possibility of purposive action and of the existence of true volition. One has only to mention the great 'demystifiers'— Darwin, Marx, and Freud—to be reminded of the reduction of man to various determinations: by the tides of evolution, by the inexorable force of economic interest, or by the biddings of libido and repressive culture. To this welter of determinisms, B. F. Skinner's onslaught on the very concept of "autonomous man" is only the most recent and most visible.

Hyperboredom is the escalating apprehension of the void; the nihilism of the masses; the largely unconscious, unacknowledged sense that the bottom has fallen out of the world; a mass echo of Nietzsche's "ich habe meine Gründe vergessen," without, however, even so much as the awareness of that lapse of memory. It of course particularly affects the young, and Novak's analysis could only be criticized in that it seems to attribute too general an awareness of what is occurring:

> Many in the younger generation . . . feel the form of consciousness of the civilization they inherit as a foreign object. Many do not yet see other forms with which to replace them. In the ensuing formlessness, they taste the experience of nothingness. Without an image by which to shape themselves, how do they know how to make sense of their experience, or who they are?[72]

Things (and Man) that had their meaning and significance for so long in their existence as an *Imago* or as an *analogon* of the Divine, and that had in the classical era at least a defined position in a taxonomic grid, have of late just fallen apart.[73] A rose, sometime symbol of the Blessed Virgin, passed in the Linnaean scheme into a plant belonging to the genus *Rosaceae;* in the twentieth century, "rose is a rose is a rose."

> What held the bones together? Not belief
> Not anything he could probe, no ligament god . . .
> He must have heard the harmony, but he swore
> Time talked to him in separated sounds,
> He took them as they came and loved them singly—
> Each one, he parried, perfect within bounds.
> As for the burden's end, the tune's direction—
> He smiled, he was content with disconnection.[74]

"No ligament god," and hence no ulterior or exterior significance for Man, so that Lévi-Strauss's program is a logical extension: "The ultimate goal of the human sciences is not to constitute but to dissolve man," with, as the ultimate objective of the exact sciences, "the reintegration of culture in nature and finally of life within the whole of its physico-chemical conditions . . . understanding life as a function of inert matter."[75] In the degree that this program has been realized, in a world that no longer provides man with meaning for himself or it, the natural response for man is boredom, just as the natural response to what threatens his existence is fear. It is not just a subjective reaction—the world *is* boring.

It is an irony that, just as the 'self' was coming to be hailed as the new core of meaning;[76] its independent status came to be assailed as the previous meaning nexus—revealed religion—had been in earlier times. With the discrediting of the only two centers of meaning that seem possible, culture and the self, it has become difficult to see how any satisfying organizing principle can be discovered that would endow our existence with the kind of significance that alone can rescue us from, as Rieff puts it, "our present temporarily schizoid existence in the two cultures— vacillating between dead purposes and deadly devices to escape boredom,"[77] the one leading to the other!

The crucial question is, then, How, if at all, is the moral energy, the positive counterpart to, and antidote against, boredom to be generated?

NOTES

1. Karl Mannheim, *Diagnosis of Our Time* (London: Kegan Paul, 1943), p. 25. Berger sees it as a crisis leading "to a vertigo, a metaphysical agoraphobia before the endless overlapping horizons of one's possible being"; *Invitation to Sociology*, p. 77.

2. Nietzsche's contemporary, Simmel, in seeing a never-ending antinomy between life and form, considered that it was no longer against any particular form or forms that life now revolted, but against form *tantum*, against the *principle* of form. See F. Pappenheim, *The Alienation of Modern Man* (New York: Monthly Review Press, 1959), p. 21.

3. The Trojan Horse was of course, full of Greeks, and among them the greatest. As Thielicke comments, in relation to the choral ode in Sophocles' *Antigone* that begins "Numberless are the world's wonders, but none/More wonderful than man": "It would appear that we have a first suggestion of a line leading inevitably to secularization, to emancipation from the gods of Hades, to a concept of man that is oriented downward" (Helmut Thielicke, *Nihilism* [New York: Schocken, 1969], p. 109). In his study of the medieval development of the concept of alienation, Gerhart Ladner writes of how "no man was as conscious of the potentialities of the beginning disintegration of the relation of man to the divine order as the greatest mystic of the Middle Ages, St. Bernard of Clairvaux." He relates this nascent disintegration to Gottfried of Strassburg's Tristan, whose "life and love take their course against the background of an order which has lost all true coherence." Later on, Ladner draws attention to the "irrational and antinomian dangers which accompanied the new consciousness of love and sexuality," and to the "internal disorder of the human person [which] had become a common phenomenon" by the fourteenth century, "a new kind of alienation." Gerhart B. Ladner, "Homo Viator: Medieval Ideas on Alienation and Order," *Speculum*, 42 (1967), pp. 233–259, passim.

4. Frederick Copleston, *A History of Philosophy*, vol. 3, part 3 (New York: Doubleday & Co., Image Books, 1963), p. 21.

5. Ibid. Cf. Dom Knowles, who ends the epilogue of *The Evolution of Medieval Thought* by declaring that "with the death of William of Ockham and his peers a great fabric of thought and an ancient outlook on philosophy as a single common way of viewing the universe gradually disappeared and gave place, after two centuries in which pure philosophy was in eclipse, to the new outlook and varied ways of the modern world" (David Knowles, *The Evolution of Medieval Thought* [New York: Random House, Vintage Books, 1962], p. 340).

6. Ockham and his disciples and successors were far from seeing the way their thought was tending in the long run, and it soon became to a large extent enmeshed in what Erasmus called "the wall of scholastic definitions, arguments, corollaries, implicit and explicit propositions," so that "The methods our scholastics pursue only render more subtle these subtlest subtleties; for you will escape from a labyrinth more quickly than from the tangle of Realists, Nominalists, Thomists, Albertists, Occamists, Scotists." But the wedge *had* been driven in, albeit as yet only the thin end! (Desiderius Erasmus, *The Praise of Folly*, cited in Jacob Bronowski and Bruce Mazlish, *The Western Intellectual Tradition* [New York: Harper & Row, 1960], p. 69.) There is still a tendency to perceive the shift as affecting only the intelligentsia. Brookes, writing in 1958, for example, sees "anomie [as] an occupational disease of the intellectual, [for whom] the value-conflicts which elsewhere are muffled by tradition and rationalisation, by inertia and impatience, become articulate. To him are revealed the hollowness of the *common certainty*." R. H. Brookes, "The Anatomy of Anomie" *Political Science* p. 47. emphasis added.

7. Hampshire puts it nicely: "In any society the concepts and forms of a language, together with the forms of popular art, combine to fix in a stereotype the resemblances in appearance which we suppose at any one time that everyone at any time must naturally notice" (Stuart Hampshire, *Thought and Action* [New York: Viking Press, 1959[, p. 33).

8. Thomas Kuhn, *The Structure of Scientific Revolutions* (Chicago: University of Chicago Press, 1970), p. 77. These developments radically undermined three fundamental *authorities:* the papacy, kingship,and the senses.

9. Blaise Pascal, *Pensées* (Baltimore: Penguin Books, 1966), p. 46.

10. Ibid.

11. Ibid., p. 47. Cf. the more cynical Montaigne: "The laws of conscience, that we pretend to be derived from nature, proceed from custom" (Michel de Montaigne, *The Complete Works*, trans. Donald M. Frame [Stanford, Calif.: Stanford University Press, 1948], p. 83).

12. Raymond Aron, *Main Currents in Sociological Thought* (Garden City, N.Y.: Doubleday & Co., Anchor Books, 1970), 2:3.

13. Michel Foucault, *The Order of Things* (New York: Random House, Vintage Books, 1973), p. 43.

14. Ibid., p. 63.

15. Ibid., p. 34. This idea was expressed in the early days of the Church by Saint Irenaeus: "Nihil cavum neque sine signum apud Deum" (*Adversus Haereses*, cited by William Gaddis, *The Recognitions* [New York: Avon Books, 1974], epigraph).

16. Foucault, *Order of Things*, pp. 29–34 passim.

17. Ibid., p. 43.

18. William Shakespeare, *As You Like It*, act 2, sc. 1, lines 16–17.

19. Matthieu Casalis, "Hermeneutics, 'Death of God' and Dissolution of the 'Subject'", (unpublished paper, University of New Mexico), p. 2.

20. Shakespeare, *Troilus and Cressida*, act 1, sc. 3, lines 82–108.

21. Ibid., act 2, sc. 2, 52.

22. Walter Kaufman, *Existentialism from Dostoevsky to Sartre* (New York: World Publishing Co., Meridian Books, 1956), p. 22.

23. H. J. C. Grierson, ed., *The Poems of John Donne* (Oxford: Oxford University Press, 1912), 1:316.

24. Ibid., "An Anatomie of the World: The First Anniversary." There is a striking resonance of these lines in Auden's poem, "Christmas, 1940," referred to above. Writing of "the bloom and buzz of a confessed collapse," he continues, "our strands of private order are dissolved/and lost our routes to self-inheritance,/Position and Relation are dismissed,/An epoch's Providence is quite worn out,/The lion of Nothing chases about./ . . . The sacred auras fade from well and wood,/The great geometries enclose our lives/In fields of normal enmity no more" (W. H. Auden, *The Collected Poetry* [New York: Random House, 1945], pp. 119–20).

25. Charles Monroe Coffin, *John Donne and the New Philosophy* New York: Humanities Press, 1958), pp. 252–53, 258, chap. 15 passim.

26. Friedrich Nietzsche, *The Will to Power* (New York: Random House, Vintage Books, 1968), p. 8.

27. William Butler Yeats, "The Second Coming," in *The Collected Poems of W. B. Yeats* (New York: Macmillan, 1956), p. 185.

28. E. A. Burtt, *The Metaphysical Foundations of Modern Physical Science* (London: Routledge & Kegan Paul, 1932), pp. 56–57.

29. William James, *The Essential Writings*, ed. Bruce Wilshire (New York: Harper & Row, 1971), p. 31.

30. Ibid., p. 368.

31. Ibid., p. 369.

32. Ibid., p. 366.

33. Ibid., p. 36.

34. T. Kuhn, *Structure of Scientific Revolutions*, p. 71.

35. Pascal, *Pensées*, p. 154. As Heller wrote in relation to Rilke ("the poet of a world, the philosopher of which is Nietzsche"): "Its formations evade all traditional systesm of cartography [an interesting echo of the Discoveries!] *Doubt has dislodged all certainties . . .* It is a world in which the order of correspondences is violently disturbed. We can no longer be sure that we love the lovable and abhor the detestable. Good does no good and evil no harm" (Erich Heller, *The Disinherited Mind* [Cleveland: World Publishing Co., 1959], p. 172, emphasis added).

36. René Descartes, *Discourse on Method*, trans. Laurence Lafleur (New York: Bobbs-Merrill, 1950), p. 12, emphasis added.

37. Ibid., p. 11. The sharp-eyed Pascal did not fail to spot Descartes's drift. "I cannot forgive Descartes," he wrote. "In all his philosophy he would have been willing to dispense with God. But he had to make him a fillip to set the world in motion; beyond this he had no further need of God" (*Pensées*, p. 77).

38. Bronowski and Mazlish, *Western Intellectual Tradition*, p. 245.

39. Nietzsche, *Will to Power:* "In the natural sciences (meaninglessness); causalism, mechanism. . . . Lawfulness an entr'acte, a residue" (p. 44).

40. T. Kuhn, *Structure of Scientific Revolutions*, p. 121.

41. Cf. Ernest Gellner, *The Legitimation of Belief* (London: Cambridge University Press, 1974). The present work argues against Gellner's belief that the world "in its natural state . . . is suffused with 'meaning', purpose, sensitivity," and that we are at present in the midst of what he calls the "Second Secularization," in which these are being eliminated. Gellner is concerned above all with, in his words, "the hump of cognition," with "the sources, nature

and authority of *the* [his emphasis] transition to effective knowledge," but he is forced by his assumption into arguing in effect that there were two transitions, one from a religious to a naturalist view of the world, and a second from the latter view, in which the world still "speaks with a human voice, . . . dovetails with our life . . . responds like a person," to one in which cognitive advance brings dehumanization (p. 196).

42. Mircea Eliade, *The Sacred and the Profane* (New York: Harcourt, Brace, & World, 1959), p. 51. Camus has pointed out that Nietzsche made "the paradoxical but significant conclusion . . . that God [had] been killed by Christianity, in that Christianity [had] secularized the sacred" (Albert Camus, *The Rebel* [New York: Random House, Vintage Books, 1956], p. 69).

43. Karl Jaspers, *Man in the Modern Age* (New York: Doubleday & Co., Anchor Books, 1957), p. 20.

44. Nietzsche, *Will to Power,* p. 7.

45. Ibid., p. 20.

46. Ibid., p. 331.

47. Robert Nisbet, "The Twilight of Authority," *The Public Interest,* Spring 1969, p. 6.

48. Robert Nisbet, *History of the Idea of Progress* (New York: Basic Books, 1980), pp. 349–51.

49. Ernest Schachtel, *Metamorphosis* (New York: Basic Books, 1959), p. 183. See also Dennis Gabor, *Inventing the Future* (London: Secker and Warburg, 1963)

50. Aristotle, *The Nichomachean Ethics* (Harmondsworth, Eng.: Penguin, 1969), bk. 10, chap. 7.

51. Josef Pieper, *Leisure: The Basis of Culture* (New York: Random House, 1963), pp. 42–54.

52. Lewis Mumford, *The Pentagon of Power* (New York: Harcourt Brace Jovanovich, 1964), p. 342.

53. William Simon and John H. Gagnon, "The Anomie of Affluence," *American Journal of Sociology* 82:356–77.

54. W. H. Auden, *The Enchafèd Plain* (New York: Random House, Vintage Books, 1967), pp. 36–37. Not that coasting along will solve the problem. In the words of Tennyson, which Auden cites, "God help me! save I take my part/Of danger on the roaring sea,/a devil rises in my heart/Far worse than death to me." One can scarcely fail to be reminded of Simone Weil's remark: "Risk is an essential need of the soul. The absence of risk produces a type of boredom which paralyzes in a different way from fear, but almost as much" (*The Need for Roots* [New York: Harper & Row, 1971], p. 34).

55. Martin C. Marty, *The Modern Schism* (New York: Harper & Row, 1969), p. 10. Cf. Philip Rieff, *The Triumph of the Therapeutic* (New York: Harper & Row, 1966):" constituencies already converted in all but name" (p. 18).

56. Nisbet, *Twilight of Authority,* p. 6.

57. Nietzsche saw this quite clearly ninety years ago: "When I think of the craving to do something, which continually tickles and spurs those millions of young Europeans who cannot endure their boredom and themselves, then I realize that they must have a craving to suffer and to find in their suffering a probable reason for action, for deeds. Neediness is needed [*Not ist nötig*]!" (*The Gay Science* [New York: Random House, Vintage Books, 1974], 1:56). The last phrase vividly recalls that which Tolstoy makes about his heroine's "desire for desires" in *Anna Karenina.*

58. Exod. 31:18.

59. Cf. Baudelaire's apposition in the title of his group of poems, "Spleen et l'idéal."

60. Hermann Hesse, *Steppenwolf* (New York: Holt, Rinehart & Winston, 1963), p. 22. "The old gods are growing old," as Durkheim remarked, "and others are not yet born. . . .

But this state of incertitude and confused agitation cannot last forever . . . there is no reason for believing that humanity is incapable of inventing new ones" (*The Elementary Forms of the Religious Life,* trans. J. W. Swain [London: George Allen & Unwin, 1964], pp. 427–28). The following chapter will examine the soundness of this confident assertion.

61. G. W. F. Hegel, *Phenomenology of Mind,* trans. J. B. Baillie (New York: Harper & Row, 1969), p. 75. A century and a half later, two sociologists writing of similar interregnums described how "words and deeds fail to give, and boredom overcomes many who feel weary of uninspiring days. Others crave forgetfulness and intoxication, and still others see the day of judgment in a sinful age which thus comes to its doom" (Hans Gerth and C. Wright Mills, *Character and Social Structure* [New York: Harcourt, Brace & World, 1964], p. 430).

62. Rainer Maria Rilke, *Duino Elegies* (New York: W. W. Norton & Co., 1963), p. 62.

63. "Die Enterbte" (the homeless ones), as Nietzsche called them in *The Gay Science;* "the outsiders" of Colin Wilson's book, *The Outsiders* (New York: Dell Publishing Co., Delta Books, 1956); Walker Percy's "castaways, who await the message in the bottle" (*The Message in the Bottle* [New York: Farrar, Straus & Giroux, 1975]). To Heller, Rilke and Nietzsche represent "the spiritually disinherited mind of Europe . . . dispossessed of all spiritual certainties," and it is his belief that when a culture lacks an "all pervasive sense of truth . . . the 'real order' has to be 'created' where there is no intuitive conviction that it exists" (Heller, *Disinherited Mind,* p. 170).

64. T. S. Eliot, *Collected Poems, 1909–1935* (New York: Harcourt, Brace & Co., 1936), p. 101.

65. Nietzsche, *Gay Science,* p. 182.

66. "The death of God is not something that has happened to God," as Rubenstein so well put it. "It has happened to us" (R. L. Rubenstein, *Morality and Eros [New York: McGraw-Hill Book Co., 1970], p. 10).

67. Friedrich Nietzsche, *Beyond Good and Evil* (New York: Random House, Vintage Books, 1966), p. 242, my translation and emphasis.

68. "No moral terms of acceptance," he continues a little later, "are any longer available, but neither are any moral terms of rejection." This "banalization of old values and the failure to create new and viable ones," has led, he believes, to the "absence of any moral order of belief" (C. Wright Mills, *Power, Politics and People* [London: Oxford University Press, 1963], pp. 332–33).

69. Nietzsche, *Will to Power,* p. 13.

70. Quoted in Bruce Wilshire, *Romanticism and Evolution* (New York: G. P. Putnam's Songs, Capricorn Books, 1968), p. 28.

71. Sigmund Freud, *Gesammelte Schriften* (Leipsig: International psychoanalytische verlag, 1924–34), 10:352.

72. Michael Novak, introduction to *Nihilism,* by Thielicke, p. 14. Elsewhere he writes of boredom as "the first taste of nothingness . . . the discovery that everything is a game" (*The Encounter with Nothingness* [New York: Harper & Row, 1970], p. 6).

73. H. G. Wells took a catastrophic view of this disintegration: "A frightful queerness has come into life. Hitherto events have been held together by a certain logical consistency, as the heavenly bodies have been held together by the golden cord of gravitation. Now it is as if the cord had vanished and everything is driven anyhow, anywhere at a steadily increasing velocity . . . The writer is convinced that there is no way out, or around, or through the impasse. It is the end" (quoted in Reinhold Niebuhr, *Faith and History* [New York: Charles Scribner's Sons, 1949], p. 163.

74. Mark Van Doren, "No Faith," in *A Comprehensive Anthology of American Poetry,* ed. Conrad Aiken (New York: The Modern Library, 1944), p. 406.

75. Claude Lévi-Strauss, *The Savage Mind* (Chicago: University of Chicago Press, 1966),

pp. 247–48. William James, decades before Heidegger, rejected materialism precisely because it "denies reality to the objects of almost all the impulses which we most cherish," and he pointed to the "intensely *objective* reference which lies in fear." To him "an enraptured man and a dreary-feeling man are not simply aware of their subjective states; if they were, the force of their feelings would all evaporate. Both believe there is outward cause why they should feel as they do: either, 'It is a glad world! how good life is!' or, 'What a loathsome tedium is existence.'" William James, *The Essential Writings*, ed. Bruce Wilshire. (New York: Harper and Row, 1971), pp. 35–36, emphasis added.

76. Yeats's poem, "A Prayer for My Daughter," is a touching memorial to this view: "The soul recovers radical innocence/And learns at last that it is self-delighting/Self-appeasing, self-affrighting,/And that *its own sweet will is Heaven's will*" (*Collected Poems*, p. 187). Joseph Campbell is among those who still believe that a source of meaning can be found in the self. Having observed that "all norms are in flux, so that the individual is thrown . . . back upon himself, into the inward sphere of his own becoming," he concludes that "today there are no horizons, no mythogenetic zones," and then immediately corrects himself by adding, "or, rather, *the mythogenetic zone is the individual heart*" (*The Masks of God: Creative Mythology* [New York: Viking Press, 1968], p. 677, emphasis added).

77. Rieff, *Triumph of the Therapeutic, p. 11*.

5 • The Future of Meaning

How did it come about that beings take precedence everywhere and lay claim to every "is" while that which is not a being is understood as Nothing, though it is Being itself, and remains forgotten?

Martin Heidegger

If it is the collapse of meaning that has led to the growth of hyper-boredom, forecasts about its further proliferation or decline must depend upon a notion of just what it is that endows cultures with meaning in the first place. What makes this essential is the fact that whatever else is postulated as the origin of the self, the individual locus of meaning, its springs are deep in society. Man, that is, is a creature shaped to a very considerable extent, unlike the rest of the animal kingdom, by external forces—his culture, his society, the 'others'. A general attenuation or general failure of meaning cannot, therefore, be simply a matter of individual psychology; it must be primarily a function of a culturewide breakdown and thus of a metaphysical crisis.

The basis from which an individual derives a sense of his own, and the world's, meaning is the perception that he has of coherence, the sense of a center. This sense endows his existence with weight, with a sense of the necessity of things (as distinct from a feeling of their mere contingency). Things are not random, haphazard, fortuitous; they form a fundamental gestalt, however little of the pattern may presently be visible or intelligible. Neither he nor they are de trop. The world has a unity, even if there are discordant elements, and this overall assurance is enough to enable him to experience himself, except for occasional lapses, as 'making sense'. The nature of such centers, the principle of coherence, does not itself seem to matter. They can be, and have been, astonishingly varied, but despite their immense differences, each may have proven effective for centuries or millennia in binding men to each other and to existence. And yet, looking at them from outside, it has to be admitted that Harry Stack Sullivan was right in describing each of them as being "a wonderful congeries having anything but a common central principle." As he said, even if one were born with the developed genius of an Einstein, one would still

> have to learn the culture because it is not capable of being understood; that is, you cannot see how it necessarily hangs together because it doesn't necessarily hang together—it falls apart.[1]

In other words, cultures cannot be understood as rational constructs for the simple reason that they were not brought into being through any process of logic or ratiocination. Their acceptance as purveying meaning cannot then derive primarily or in the first instance from their satisfying man's reason. Philip Rieff put it succinctly when he wrote that

> a culture survives principally . . . by the power of its institutions to bind and loose man in the conduct of their affairs with reasons which sink so deeply into the self that they become commonly and implicitly understood.[2]

In speaking of 'reasons', Rieff is clearly not referring to rational grounds but to that nexus of prerational, prereflective attitudes and beliefs which, while they do not "hang together" extrinsically, come to be felt to do so intrinsically, even in the face of rational criticism, even to the extent that in any clash between the two it will be rationality that is impugned rather than they. As Sullivan went on to point out, it is precisely that part of the culture incorporated into himself by the human animal which is *not* "run through the consciousness . . . the unwitting part of it,"[3] which enables the culture to continue (to which it is necessary to add here, in order to avoid any suggestion of prejudging the issue, "at least until our own epoch").

It is rather as if nature, in denying us exact instincts, gave us, or made us able to develop, social systems as a substitute instinctual exoskeleton to protect us against the pressure of infinite possibility. The Dutch sociologist, Jan Romein, after analyzing a broad cross section of human societies, found it possible to distill from them an ideal type, a matrix that he called the Common Human Pattern, in which life is not something to be realized by the individual but a gift of god, gods, spirits, or fate. It is something that happens to you . . . The authority of the gods, or the father, or the teacher, or the book (Scriptures, Koran) is the cornerstone of the CHP and will never be questioned. It provides the world with stability and shields it from the threats of chaos or anomie.[4]

Nurtured in the CHP, the individual self is as firmly centered, as fully assured of meaning, as the society itself. Both go deep and remain for all intents and purposes invisible. To one of its members his society *is* society, all others mere aggregates; to him all men outside his group are mere hominids, barbarians. The self, in other words, is just an individual variation on what the culture regards as human nature, something about whose general definition there neither is, nor could be, any problem. The terms and content of the definition have as we know varied from society to society, even from group to group within a particular society, but that there was some objective reality corresponding to the term 'human nature' (that is the *correct* view of man) has not been subject to general doubt until relatively recent times. This means that it has always been possible for men to have inauthentic selves, to be untrue to their perception of their own nature as human beings. The Christian doctrine of sin, for example, is that man, by an act of will, turns his back on that divine element which is his most fundamental being. All the so-called deadly sins, the *vitia capitalia*, are considered to derive their gravity from the willful turning away. Acedia, anglice 'sloth',[5] which has been equated in this study with hyperboredom, was an individual possibility because each man had the freedom to act against his own nature, but since he did so within a society that had no doubts of its own view of the truth or of its own definition of human nature, such acts served to reinforce the norm rather than to bring it into question. Hyperboredom, in this context, was a personal act of defiance, an individual psychological aberration, a sin.

However, as a previous chapter sought to chronicle, the authenticity of Western culture and its definition of man have been subject to heavy and increasingly numerous and varied assaults in the last few centuries. Knowledge has poured in and skepticism has mounted. A dramatic indication of the erosion of the self-evident quality of the culture was given in Scheler's famous statement of over half a century ago that "we are the first age in which man has become utterly and unconditionally problematic to himself, in which he no longer knows who he is, but at the same time *knows that* he does not know."[6]

It is possible, and not uncommon, for this development to be viewed as an emancipation from the straitjacket of culture, and to regard what Durkheim spoke of as the *dérèglement* of modern man—his unboundedness by any compelling norms—in the light of a liberation from hitherto unrecognized and unnecessary subliminal restrictions. On the other hand, it may be, as Heidegger maintained, that this 'emancipation' constitutes the opening of a gap between man and Being. However, it is not so much, as Heidegger thought, that man is forgetful of Being as that, removed from his hitherto normal, symbiotic relationship with Being, in which the only self that all but a few could develop was a variation on an Us-self, man has lost his sense of the location and nature of Being.[7] Like one forced out of Plato's cave into the full light of reality, his eyes are dazzled and his mind confused. Man no longer knows what it is to be man because he knows too much about what man can be. He finds himself in a world confronted not with one alternative interpretation of the cosmos, but with an indefinite and growing array of alternative explanations, all loudly, brilliantly, and insistently urged on every side. "One interpretation has collapsed," wrote Nietzsche in 1887, "but because it was considered *the* interpretation it now seems as if there were no meaning at all in existence, as if everything were vain."[8]

Since then man has seen even the reassuringly firm world of nineteenth-century natural science dissolve, atoms breaking into subatomic particles, and those into insubstantial, scarcely conceivable fields of force and mathematical abstractions. With truth, it seems to have become like a slippery marble: the harder one presses it, the faster and farther it shoots from one's grasp. Knowledge and reality have come to seem related to each other—if at all—asymptotically. It is all too clear that multitudes now make the "tremendous generalization" that Nietzsche himself viewed as pathological, namely "the inference that there is no meaning at all . . . that there is no truth, that there is no absolute nature of things nor a 'thing in itself.'[9] Whether this inference is true or false, the fact that it is made and perhaps even more important, felt, is incontestable and is a major obstacle to the reemergence of a sense of meaning in human existence on both a social and an individual level, a revival without which hyperboredom is certain to continue and to extend its ravages.

Any pluralistic society faces the same problem, that of establishing, as Berger and Luckman phrase it, "a stable symbolic canopy for the *entire* society." They go on to point out that "specific procedures of universe-maintenance become necessary when the symbolic universe has become a *problem*"[10] But it is one thing to say that the maintenance is necessary and quite another to suppose that it is possible in all circumstances. Even when the number of alternative universes in major competition with the official one was relatively small, as in the latter days of the Roman Empire, maintenance proved unsuccessful no matter how many times the emperors proclaimed the restoration of the status quo. The present difficulty of maintaining—or revising—Western man's universe is compounded by the existence of *numerous* radically different alternatives that defy all efforts to spread any common "symbolic canopy" over them, and by the even more corrosive awareness pointed to by Scheler: man's knowledge that "he does not know."

Even to bring the "symbolic universe" into consciousness and to submit it to rational examination is to run the risk Sullivan pointed to in dealing with what he called 'sublimation'—the process of enculturation by which men are brought to transmute their energies into approved activity and belief—namely, that "if you tell people they can sublimate, they can't sublimate."[11] Which is to say that, if enough doubts of the ontological validity of a culture and its views of man are raised by evidence of its varieties, its shifts, its 'rational' absurdities, and by the contention that all religions are ideologies, epiphenomena of a given infrastructure—if, in a word, the critical mass of a people come to *suppose* that they have been shown how people come to believe, then they will not be able to believe in belief any more.[12]

In analyzing the process by which man becomes bound by societal forms that were themselves made by man, Berger and Luckman make use of the Marxian concept of *Verdinglichung,* the perception that while man is author of the human 'world' he in turn reifies it and becomes able to 'forget' the fact of his authorship and to apprehend his society as a "non-human facticity."[13] But this is of course to suggest a much too deliberate process. It may well be that man is the author, but until recently at least he has not been *conscious* of himself acting in this role—as proofreader, editor, or even publisher, perhaps, but not as author. If he has been 'sublimating', he has not been aware of it, and the question now arises whether he can be "bound and loosed" by "reasons" of which he has become aware.

This presents evident difficulties, for the knowledge man now seems to have attained gives rise in our age to the profoundly subversive suspicion that at last the trick of culture has been exposed, that man has finally escaped the inauthentic world of bad faith.[14] This is really no more than an elaboration of a view going back at least as far as Pascal and Montaigne, but the other, modern edition is highly significant: the "reasons" that Rieff refers to are being dredged up in full view of a massive audience, which stands around and witnesses what they fondly believed to be basic and immutable truth being brought to the surface apparently stamped "Made by Man." But just what happens when the "deception" that Berger regards as a "functional imperative," or as Sullivan called it, "the unwitting part," of culture, the part that gives it its gravitational pull is, at least in the estimation of many, clearly exposed for what it is? To point out as Rieff does that "culture *must* communicate ideals, setting as *internalities* those distinctions between right actions and wrong that unite men"[15] is by no means to establish that it *can* do so after the 'trick' of sublimation is brought to consciousness. Myth, symbol, and ritual, once they are seen for what they are (or rather, are reduced to their supposed origins), and their functionings are teased out and made explicit, must inevitably lose much, if not all, of their efficacy.

Nietzsche was, of course, here first, but he made a connection between 'use and wont' and boredom that he himself did not follow up, and that has not hitherto been taken up, but that is central to the present study. "Founders of religion" were to him those who had realized the need

> to posit a particular kind of life and everyday customs that have the effect of a *disciplina voluntatis* and at the same time banish boredom—and then to bestow on this lifestyle an *interpretation* that makes it appear to be illuminated by the highest value.[16]

In other words, boredom—hyperboredom—is avoidable, at least for "the herd animal with its . . . boredom with itself,"[17] only if somebody can endow a particular "life-style" that acts as a complex of limitations with supreme, transcendent value. The clear implication, though he did not spell it out, is that in an age that finds the whole idea of objective value, and, a fortiori, supreme and transcendent value, so difficult, hyperboredom is bound to proliferate. In the degree, then, that a Nietzschean analysis of the origin of religion comes to be accepted, the way back into meaning seems progressively closed off; for if we know that man, whether identifiable by name or not, injected religious value into the world, then how shall we, finding "how the world is fabricated solely from psychological needs,"[18] be able to maintain our belief in the reality of that value? How can the process Nietzsche alleges to lie at the root of religion continue to work once man has become aware of it and can even, in our own time, watch the not always unsuccessful attempts of would-be 'founders' to put it to use?

Nietzsche's analysis may, however, be naive, even farfetched, if what we are concerned about is authentic religion rather than mere faddish cults. What if the "unwitting part," at least so far as religion and faith are concerned, comes not, as he supposes, from some human intervention, but from a radically different source? From that source, perhaps, that the Evangelist Matthew was referring to when he wrote of Christ that "he taught as one *having authority*," or, as the Greek has it, *exousia* ("out of being")? This conception of religious vision as a revelation of Being bears a striking affinity with that pre-Socratic idea of truth as *a-lethia* ("un-hiddenness," "dis-coveredness") which Heidegger revived in his writings. Truth is no conquest of the will to power, but a quasi-passive attunement of man to Being—the "letting-go" of the Taoist, the "abandonment" or "releasement" of Meister Eckhardt, the "indwelling" of Dilthey,the "tacit knowledge" of Michael Polanyi. Man does not, and cannot, install meaning in existence; it is not his to bestow. Instead, man has access to a realm of meaning through "primordial" thinking, more akin to a direct experience of reality, but he may "fall away" from this authentic contact through absorption in "calculative" thinking, the analytic mode of science and of everyday life. The latter tranquillizes, alienates, and scatters since it is a flight from the true self. In the Heideggerian analysis, this *Fall*, or deterioration, derives from the *Angst* caused by man's awareness of the "radical nullity and finitude of existence."[19] Man flees this nullity, represented finally by death, and he thus becomes not bored *to* death (as the usual expression has it), but bored *away from* death, because he cannot face up to the authentic possibility of his existence and thus deprives it of any meaning.

Seen in this light, the Nietzschean will to power appears both as springing from and as adding to man's forgetfulness of Being. In proportion as he struggles to master Being, it eludes his grasp. In the words Goethe put into Mephistopheles' mouth," Wer will was Lebendigs erkennen und beschreiben/Sucht zuerst den Geist herauszutreiben";[20] or as Wordsworth put it, "we murder to dissect"—not accidentally, but necessarily. Thus we have a classic dilemma for, if, as Barrett suggests in reference to Heidegger's inability to "produce that sense of Being for a new era,"

> the philosophy of the will leads to an alienation from Being, then we cannot secure that tie again by a sheer act of will. . . . The new god or gods that need to be born will come neither at our command nor by our contrivance.[21]

The "need" is, naturally, ours not theirs, and his expectation that "they" will come, *if at all* as an authentic "happening out of depths," inevitably prompts the question, Out of whose (or which) depths?

One is reminded of Durkheim's view of the sacred, and of religion, as arising out of a collective exaltation, a sacred frenzy, of which the Cult of Reason that arose during the French Revolution was an inauthentic exemplar. Today, however, we might be less prepared to confound religion with the effects of certain kinds of psychosocial phenomena, having learned caution from observing the absurdities or even satanic enormities to which such sacred frenzies can lead. No doubt mana, "an anonymous and diffused force,"[22] as Durkheim called it, is generated by any group of people, but we know too much about its destructive possibilities to be sanguine about the benign nature of "happenings" out of the "depths."

As yet, even less success has attended the efforts of those who, like Comte (the first to enunciate the idea that common beliefs are essential to the maintenance of a viable culture), sought to erect a compelling religion on the basis of 'reason'. His "religion of humanity," with society not God at its center, disappeared rapidly and almost without trace. The equally rationalistic proposal of Theodore Geiger in our own day, aiming at the elimination of all public groups based on nonrational values, and others of a similar kind, seem to have no future because of the same contradiction. The essence of this approach is the supposition that

> the technical apparatus of civilization as well as the structure of society demand . . . a shift in favor of the intellectual powers, a systematic intellectualization of the individual and his training in emotional asceticism.[23]

And it is coupled with a call for "a renunciation of collective cults of value, religion, nationalism, etc., through 'value nihilism', the philosophical exposure of the value-idea as an illusion."[24]

In fact, given the current situation, efforts to establish a compelling religion or philosophy solely on reason must evidently be self-defeating since rationality itself is implicated in the problem, at least that form of it which William James stigmatized as "vicious intellectualism," the epistemological totalitarianism that excludes any but narrowly defined 'empirically verifiable' statements from truth status. "Two excesses," as Pascal wrote, "reason excluded; nothing but reason allowed," and if the official modern tendency is toward the latter, in the form of positivism, scientism, humanism and so on, then it is perhaps not surprising that there is a corresponding efflorescence of necromancy, sorcery, witchcraft, numerology, astrology, and of outlandish cults.

The situation is strikingly reminiscent of that described by Huizinga when he wrote of some of the features of the latter days of the Roman Empire that they

> stamp the last phase of Rome's ancient greatness with inveterate frivolity. Life has become a game of culture; the ritual form persists, but the religious spirit has flown. All the deeper spiritual impulses withdraw from the culture of the surface and strike new root in the mystery religions. Finally, when Christianity cut Roman civilization off from its ritual basis, it withered rapidly.[25]

The drive toward mystery religions is paralleled in our own day, but the extreme sophistication that Western man has acquired in the centuries since Rome, and in particular his exclusionary empiricism, seem insuperable obstacles to a repetition of the earlier solution, which in any case came only in the wake of massive, century-long cultural dislocation and social collapse. Rationality appears to have played in the last century or two the part played in the declining Empire by on the one hand Christianity and on the other the barbarians, in dissolving many of the bonds of 'custom and wont', but with the crucial difference that it does not seem possible to descry any seeds being planted from which humanly satisfying 'custom and wont' could conceivably arise. Whereas Christianity was perfectly compatible with the general state of secular knowledge in the fractured culture within which it spread, any attempted revival of a traditional faith—and in a sense, any 'faith' whatever *would* be traditional, however new in detail—would fly in the face of what is popularly accepted as knowledge.

But if neither rationality nor faith (or credulity) can provide the sort of meaning that will ward off hyperboredom, then what will?

The difficulty of finding an answer is only compounded when, on closer inspection, it becomes evident that it is actually not rationality as such that lies at its root but the immense and it would seem irreversible growth in consciousness[26] and self-consciousness (reflexivity) which is dialectically related to that rationalism. The theme has received extended, even obsessive, treatment at the hands of the Rumanian expatriate, Cioran, who characterizes "civilized man [as] victim of an exacerbated consciousness." Using 'lucidity' in the sense of reflective consciousness, he writes:

> A minimum of unconsciousness is necessary if one wants to stay inside history. To act is one thing, to know one is acting is another. When lucidity invests the action, insinuates itself into it, action is undone, and, with it, prejudice, whose function consists precisely in subordinating, in enslaving consciousness to action. The man who unmasks his fictions renounces his own resources and, in a sense, himself. . . . No man concerned with his equilibrium may exceed a certain degree of lucidity and analysis. How much more this applies to a civilization, which vacillates as soon as it exposes the errors which permitted its growth and its luster, as soon as it calls into question *its own* truths![27]

Nietzsche earlier had asked the question "that seems to lie upon our tongues and yet never becomes articulate: the question whether we can consciously remain in falsehood," and had managed to answer it positively—for himself at least—through "the recognition of delusion and error as a condition of knowledge and feeling."[28] Recognizing that the growth of consciousness was a "danger" and a "disease," he wrote that "we need blindness sometimes, and must allow certain articles of faith and errors to remain untouched within us—so long as they maintain us in life."[29] But just how to persuade marvelously clear-, if narrow-, sighted modern man that he 'must' do any such thing? It is not easy to see how, or indeed why, man is to become and remain deliberately selectively 'blind', while the culture continues to urge the necessity of being intensely and universally open-eyed. What criterion of selectivity, what premiss, can be immune from conscious criticism, by which it becomes inevitably moot and ineffective? Karl Mannheim a generation ago made the observation that greater consciousness and deliberation had "completely upset the balance between conscious and unconscious forces operating in our society,"[30] but even though he saw the critical nature of the shift, his own rationalism, sensitive as it was, somehow never quite enabled him to perceive that the solutions he proposed under the general rubric "Planning for Freedom" were themselves just a little less obvious part of the "philosophy of the will." He spoke of "creating a new moral world based upon rational value appreciation,"[31] as if such a project did not beg the question, did not quite gloss over the fundamental dilemma that Blake pointed to with utmost simplicity in two brief lines:

> If the Sun and Moon should doubt
> They'd immediately go out.

If nothing is self-evident, nothing can be built upon it; and once the suspicion is abroad that nothing *is* certain, the game is up, for to the paranoid everything has become suspect, and an absolute logic of suspicion cuts him off from reality, from any certainty except that of his own nihilistic and annihilating doubt.[32]

How this came about in America is the theme of Daniel Boorstin's recent concluding volume in his trilogy *The Americans,* and in particular of book two, "The Decline of the Miraculous." Reviewing the processes and changes he has already detailed, and previewing those he is just about to deal with, he writes how,

> In America the crude intractable facts of life . . . were being dissolved. The regularities of nature, by which men knew that they were alive and were only human . . . all these were being confused. The old tricks of the miracle maker . . . become commonplace. . . . When man could accomplish miracles he began to lose his sense of the miraculous. This meant, too, a decline of common sense, and the irrelevance of the rules of thumb that had governed man since the beginning of history.

He goes on to point to *attenuation* as "the new quality of experience . . . thinner, more diluted, its sensations weaker and less poignant," and then gets to the crucial question whether after "civilization had survived man's limitations it could . . . also survive his near omnipotence?"[33]

Things from which the aura of meaning has withdrawn in this way cease to be in any profound sense 'interesting'; things in and by themselves are boring, since interest is a characterization that men bring to them, the perception that they have meaning, something they do not, of course, have for themselves or for each other. Thus, in Sartre's idea of Being as essentially and absolutely meaningless, boredom results from a prereflective awareness of that Being; and boredom, conversely, gives us direct access to, and direct awareness of, that Being as brute existence, Nothingness. But what Sartre sees as implicit in Being, others perceive as an alienation from it, so that without this sense of meaning we are cut off from our roots in Being,[34] that in which we are embedded and out of which we, and things, emerge.

It was already evident as early as Melville's time that men were "nearly all Islanders," none "acknowledging the common continent of men, but each *Isolato* living on a separate continent of his own." A century later the process is far advanced, for many, perhaps even most, men do not now even acknowledge the existence of any *continent*.[35] Gabriel Marcel wrote of man living in a "broken world," and Glenn Tinder more recently described the nature of the fracture that

> make[s] it appear that almost every contact which human beings desire or value has been weakened or broken. The enjoyment of nature is difficult and occasional; one's roots in a place are taken up or not allowed to form; possessions stand in a largely outward and merely instrumental relationship to the personality; the past is obscure and the future almost totally darkened; the more deep and satisfying contacts among persons, always difficult, have become more fragile.[36]

It seems that Man has now to try to grow his roots—such as survive—back into Being, that is, to recover contact with the source of all that he is, but whether this reversal of the natural process is possible remains to be seen. In the case of some plants, it is true, a cutting will put out roots of its own, but it can only *take* root if there is ground into which to sink them. The question is whether mankind can think its way back into the ground, the very existence, location, and nature of which is doubted, or whether the very attempt would not represent a basic contradiction, analogous to putting the cart before the horse or trying to pull oneself up by one's own bootstraps.[37]

Bruce Wilshire got to the heart of the matter when, in relation to the development of romanticism, he pointed out that "for the first time in history the primacy of *the actual* over *the possible* was being doubted.[38] Which is to say that—initially—a handful of the romantics came to believe that it could no longer be taken for granted, if at all, that the human self *is* something that fixes what human beings *are*, what they can be and do, and above all, what they *ought* to be and do. The egg comes before the chicken (and it is not any particular kind of egg); existence comes before essence, not vice versa. Since in this view man never is, but always *is to be* (to paraphrase Alexander Pope), nothing of what man should be can be deduced from what he by nature is. If Wilshire's observation is correct, and the great extension of boredom argues that it is, then the dissolution of the cultural center in recent history may well herald a major crisis and a protracted "time of troubles, already long since begun." This likelihood is strengthened by the fact that though in our day this nihilism may, in its conscious form, still be limited to those whom Riesman called the "inside dopesters"—the elite and the intelligentsia—it is being unconsciously absorbed by the masses in the processes of education, whether formal or informal. The situation resembles what would occur if we could each take control of our autonomic nervous and vascular systems. Given their immense complexities, a condition of their continuing to function is precisely our inability to get at the controls and to blunder around, with nothing but our intellects and emotions to guide; granted this access, we should soon be dead.

It might be accurate to say of man's *physical* being, "that it is self-delighting,/Self-appeasing, self-affrighting/And that its own sweet will is Heaven's will," but it was not, of course of the body that Yeats was writing, but of the soul, and in this regard it appears pretty certain by now that if there is what one might call an autonomic moral system, a Natural Law, that its demands are difficult to identify and that, to compound the problem, we are certainly much more able to get at the controls and to obscure any innate regulating mechanism by the very fact of our intervention. In this sphere we seem to many to be confronted by a dilemma much like that uncovered in the realm of physics by Heisenberg in the 1930s, namely, that our observation of 'reality' so disturbs the 'reality' we are observing that we cannot say for sure what is really real.

In seeking to reinstate meaning and to eliminate hyperboredom, man is thus up against a twofold difficulty: he cannot, on the one hand, depend for guidance about the nature of reality on anything in his own culture, befuddled as he is by a plethora of guides (and Guides) who clamor for his acceptance; and on the other, such doubts have been cast on the possibility of discerning it through introspection that the individual lacks any real confidence in the existence of any reality at all beyond that which appears to present itself to his senses, the reliability of which has also been progressively undermined. There is additionally the fact that man is to an unknown, but certainly large, extent the creator of the very 'real-

112 • *The Future of Meaning*

ity' that he generally supposes himself merely to be observing and recording, which gives rise to the fundamentally subversive suspicion that it may be, as Auden wrote that, "mirror in mirror, mirrored is all the show." Some hold on to the possibility of an Archimedean point in the moral universe that gives sufficient purchase for levering the ethical world back on to its true axis. Abraham Maslow, for example, considers that "the cure for this disease [a value interregnum] is obvious," and goes on to claim that

> we need a validated, usable system of humane values that we can believe in and devote ourselves to (be willing to die for) because they are true rather than because we are exhorted to "Believe and have faith." Such an empirically based Weltanschauung seems now to be a real possibility, at least in theoretical outline.[39]

But he does not go on to show even generally what such an "empirically based" system would look like, or how one could deduce values from facts, or what would generate the necessary passion, sense of certainty, and intensity of dedication in the mass of people.

If man's essence is his existence, if, to paraphrase Ortega y Gasset, man has no nature, only a history, then perhaps the future belongs to "Protean Man," characterized, in the words of his discoverer and/or projector, Robert Lifton, "by an interminable series of experiments and explorations, some shallow, some profound, each of which can readily be abandoned in favor of still new, psychological quests."[40] Or maybe to the "serial self" of "super-industrial man," foreseen by Alvin Toffler, who "altering his identity as he goes . . . traces a private trajectory through a world of colliding subcults . . . Again and again . . . bitter or bored, vaguely dissatisfied with 'the way things are.'"[41] In McLuhanesque fashion, such a characterological chameleon, "even when he seems most firmly plugged in to his group or tribe . . . listens, in the dark of night, to the short-wave signals of competing tribes."[42]

Toffler suggests the need for a "new theory of personality" to take account of the novel type of man already coming into existence, but he does admit that "the multiplication of life styles challenges our ability to hold the very self together."[43] In fact neither he nor Lifton really distinguishes between 'self' and 'role', and in this respect they share Erving Goffman's view that the self is nothing *but* a role, or a series of roles. The individual gives performances that create an image, and while this image is entertained concerning the individual, so that the self in imputed to him, this self does not derive from its possessor, but from the whole scene of his action. . . . The self, then, as a performed character, is not an organic thing . . . is a dramatic effect.[44]

This is a view of man that might be called post-faustian. Faust, it will be remembered, declared that

> What is portioned out to all mankind
> I shall enjoy deep in my self . . .
> And thus let my own self grow into theirs,
>   unfettered,
> Till as they are, at last I, too, am shattered.[25]

With Faust, there is still an actor, even if it is one who desires to extinguish himself in the others, but from the perspective of the preceding writers there is no danger that a man's self might be dissolved or crushed, torn apart or surrendered by his own act of will, for any such entity is a chimera. 'I' and 'we' have become 'one', or in German, *man,* and my-self has become the 'they-self' *(Das Man)* described by Heidegger. Only Toffler appears to have noticed that, as men become persuaded that they are no more than a series of performances enacted through them rather than by them, that the 'self' is no more than the sum of its performances,[46] they will fall understandably prey to the conviction that their own existence is absurd, and that of the world totally meaningless. With this will come flooding in one or the other—or a cyclic oscillation of the indications of hyperboredom—a deep, mordant indifference or a frenetic search for distraction. If the erstwhile actor becomes assimilated to his assigned role or roles, in reality becoming no more than an act-ee, then what were once perceived as acts come to be seen in their true light as mere motions, and a vacuum[47] appears at the center of each of us, a shift of perspective so radical that it can hardly fail—at least in the interim period needed for the phasing out of those raised in exploded illusions of agency—to produce a bleak, boring sense of nothingness in the wake of this fundamental de-creation.

NOTES

1. Harry Stack Sullivan, "The Illusion of Personal Individuality," *Psychiatry* 13 (1950):323. Cf. Faust's ruminating over "was die Welt/Im innersten zusammenhält." For another view, see Louis Dumont, who writes that "it is at the level of those unstated 'views' [the hidden assumptions of the culture] that the different parts of the ideology *hang together*" (emphasis added). Even though he recognizes that "in the modern world each of our particular viewpoints or specialized pursuits does not know very well—or does not know at all—what it is about," he believes that if we want to get an overall view of our culture, "we must dive to the level of the unexpressed as we would for any less 'rational society,'" supposing, it is clear, that at that level there *is* something there, or more exactly and significantly, some coherent and cohesive framework. He suggests that the antidote to "the relativism, which could conclude from diversity to unreality" (i.e., meaninglessness), is the "nonideological residue" to be found through the cultural distillation of comparative anthropological studies (*From Mandeville to Marx* [Chicago: University of Chicago Press, 1977], p. 20).

2. Philip Rieff, *The Triumph of the Therapeutic* (New York: Harper & Row, 1966), p. 2. This insight has, of course, had numerous earlier expressions. Edmund Burke, for example, insisted upon the vital power of "prejudice" and "use and wont" (*Reflections on the Revolution in France*); Friedrich Nietzsche referred to "that which creates a morality, a code of laws: the profound instinct that only automatism makes possible perfection in life and creation" (*The Will to Power*); Alfred North Whitehead wrote of his main thesis as being "that a social system is kept together by the blind force of instinctive emotions clustered around habits and prejudice" (*Symbolism: Its Meaning and Effects*); and the "habit" engendered by "the enormous flywheel of society," of which William James wrote, is a similar conception of this universal prereflexive absorption in the culture (*Principles of Psycology*).

3. Sullivan, "Illusion of Personal Individuality," p. 323. Cf. Emile Durkheim, *Suicide*. "Both spring from *society's insufficient presence in man*" (p. 258); and also, "disgust will of course follow *if the moral character of the obligation is no longer felt.* What actually matters in fact is not only that the regulation should exist, but that it should be *accepted by the conscience*" (p. 272), n. 19; all emphasis added.

4. Jan Romein, *Het Algemeen Menselijk Patroon*, cited in Anton C. Zijderveld, *The Abstract Society* (New York: Doubleday & Co., Anchor Books, 1970), pp. 66–67. William Earle refers to this concept simply as "culture . . . that instinctive sense of coherence, signification, and order *where mind is straightforward.* Its will wills the objective, divine good; its thoughts think the truth; and its arts are at one and the same time useful and in the service of the gods" ("The Future of Civilization," *Philosophy Forum* 13 [1973]:215).

5. 'Sloth' is defined in the *Catholic Moral Dictionary* as "deliberate boredom."

6. Max Scheler, "Man and History," in Max Scheler, *Man's Place in Nature* (New York: Farrar, Straus & Cudahy, 1961), translator's introduction, p. xii.

7. Cf. Nikolai Berdyaev, *The Destiny of Man* (London: Bles, 1937), p. 1: "Man has lost the power of knowing real being, has lost access to reality and been reduced to studying knowledge." Epistemology has been substituted for ontology!

8. Friedrich Nietzsche, *The Will to Power* (New York: Random House, Vintage Books, 1968), p. 35. A modern expression of this radical collapse is provided by Michael Novak: "The experience of nothingness defined. . . . *There is no one obligatory way to perceive things.* Action is problematical because no goal at all seems more valuable, more useful, or more attractive than any other . . . an experience of the formlessness at the heart of human consciousness" (Michael Novak, introduction to *Nihilism*, by Helmut Thielicke [New York: Schocken Books, 1969], p. 3).

9. Nietzsche, p. 14.

10. Peter Berger and Thomas Luckman, *The Social Construction of Reality* (New York: Doubleday & Co., Anchor Books, 1967), pp. 86, 105.

11. Sullivan, "Illusion of Personal Individuality," p. 323.

12. Cf. Thielicke's remark that "once the gods have been exploded, we can never return to that former innocence" (Thielicke, *Nihilism*, p. 94). This reference to the loss of 'innocence', the source of our certitude, reminds one of Yeats's lines from "A Prayer for My Daughter"—"How but in custom and ceremony/Are innocence and beauty born?"—which convey the same belief that innocence and beauty (the innate affinity that exists between our own nature and being as such) can only be realized in a society in which life is governed by immemorial and largely unreflective ways, a society such as those described by Romein as falling within the CHP. In "The Two Trees," a poem he wrote a quarter of a century earlier, in 1893, Yeats gave a poet's piercingly exact vision of the crucial shift already under way, but so far largely unrecognized, from what he called "the great ignorant leafy ways" of the "holy tree" to "unresting thought":

> Beloved, gaze in thine own heart,
> The holy tree is growing there . . .
> The surety of its hidden root
> Has planted quiet in the night . . .
>
> Gaze no more in the bitter glass
> The demons, with their subtle guile,
> Lift up before us when they pass . . .
> For all things turn to barrenness
> In the dim glass the demons hold,
> The glass of outer weariness,
> Made when God slept in times of old.
> There, through the broken branches, go
> The ravens of unresting thought.

(William Butler Yeats, *Selected Poems* [London: Macmillan, 1959], pp. 47–48.) Cioran calls this experience the "fall into time," in which "the living man perceives existence everywhere; once awakened, once he is no longer *nature*, he begins to discern the false in the apparent, the apparent in the real, and ends by suspecting the very idea of reality." "We live," he adds later, "only by lack of knowledge. Once we *know*, we are at odds with everything" (E. M. Cioran, *The Fall into Time* [Chicago: Quadrangle, 1970], p. 155).

13. Berger and Luckman, *Social Construction of Reality*, p. 89.

14. Berger (following in Nietzsche's footsteps) goes so far as to say that "deception and self-deception are at the very heart of social reality. The deception inherent in social structure is a *functional* imperative. Society can maintain itself *only* if its fictions (its 'as if' character, to use Hans Vaihinger's term) are accorded ontological status by at least some of its members some of the time" (Peter Berger, *Invitation to Sociology* [Harmondsworth, Eng.: Penguin, 1963], pp. 166–67).

15. Rieff, *Triumph of the Therapeutic*, p. 4, emphasis added.

16. Friedrich Nietzsche, *The Gay Science* (New York: Random House, Vintage Books, 1974), p. 296. Elsewhere, he pointed to what he saw as the "inveterate mendaciousness" of morality, and to the "needs for untruth" implanted in us by centuries of moral interpretation. To him, and of course through him, "the shabby origin of these values" was becoming clear; "the universe seems to have lost value, seems 'meaningless' "—but this was "only a transitional stage" (*Will to Power*, pp. 10–11).

17. *The Gay Science*, p. 295.

18. *Will to Power*, p. 13.

116 • *The Future of Meaning*

19. John Macquarrie, *Martin Heidegger* (Richmond, Va.: John Knox Press, 1968), p. 29.

20. "In our very desire to understand and describe a living being we first of all try to get rid of the life" (Johann Wolfgang von Goethe, *Faust: Der Tragödie Erster Teil.* Studierzimmer, lines 1936–37). C. S. Lewis was pointing to the same dilemma when he wrote of "analytical understanding" that "perhaps in the nature of things, [it] must always be a basilisk which kills what it sees and only sees by killing" (C. S. Lewis, *The Abolition of Man* [New York: Macmillan, 1947], p. 90).

21. William Barrett, *Time of Need* (New York: Harper & Row, 1972), p. 376. Heidegger (from whose writings Barrett took the title of his book) was himself reported in the 9 May, 1976 issue of *Der Spiegel* as having said that nothing was to be hoped for "all simply human thoughts and strivings. Only a god can save us." A new god, presumably, since under Nietzsche's influence he had long before this quite given up his earlier, self-confessed function as a "Christian theologian" (Letter from Heidegger to Karl Löwith, 19 August 1921, cited in Walter Kaufman, *Discovering the Mind* [New York: McGraw-Hill Book Co., 1980], 2:170–71, 193).

22. Emile Durkheim, *The Elementary Forms of the Religious Life*, trans. Joseph Ward Swain (London: George Allen & Unwin, 1964), p. 194.

23. Theodor Geiger, *On Social Order and Mass Society*, trans. Robert E. Peck (Chicago: University of Chicago Press, 1969), p. 187.

24. Ibid., p. 237.

25. Johan Huizinga, *Homo Ludens* (Boston: Beacon Press, 1955), p. 178.

26. 'Consciousness' is used here as indicating the obverse of what Earle refers to as 'culture,' As he points out, the effect of civilization, of mind "consciously reflective upon culture [is] to place all these values [the true, the good, and the beautiful] within quotation marks" (Future of Civilization," p. 215). Earle's thought owes much to Kierkegaard, who, under the pseudonym Johannes Climacus, wrote that "the possibility of doubt lies in consciousness, whose very essence is to be a kind of contradiction or opposition." *Johannes Climacus or, De Omnibus Dubitandum Est.* Trans. T. H. Croxall (Stanford: Stanford University Press, 1958), p. 148. See also Daniel O'Connor, "The Phenomena of Boredom," *Journal of Existentialism*, 7 (1967), pp. 381–399, and Josiah Thompson, who refers to this doubt rather memorably as "the wound of consciousness." *Kierkegaard* (New York: Alfred A. Knopf, 1973), p. 166.

27. E. M. Cioran, *The Temptation to Exist* (Chicago: Quadrangle, 1973), p. 55.

28. Cited in Hans Vaihinger, *The Philosophy of "As-If"* (New York: Barnes & Noble, 1968), pp. 345–46.

29. Ibid, p. 346, n. 1.

30. Karl Mannheim, *Diagnosis of Our Time* (London: Kegan Paul, 1943), p. 22.

31. Ibid., p. 24.

32. Cf. Zijderveld, in analyzing "the intrinsic relationship between meaning, reality and freedom. . . . He is free who experiences social reality as meaningful and who knows his position and identity as traditional and taken-for-granted qualities. *The moment doubt is cast upon this meaning and reality freedom becomes a problem*" (*Abstract Society*, p. 139, emphasis added).

33. Daniel J. Boorstin, *The Americans: The Democratic Experience* (New York: Random House, 1973), pp. 305–8 passim.

34. Saint Anselm's "credo ut intelligam" is echoed in our own epoch by, for example, Alan Tate's "man is a creature that in the long run has got to believe in order to know" (Alan Tate, *The Forlorn Demon* [Chicago: Henry Regnery Co., 1953], p. 7).

35. The distance that Western man had traversed in two centuries is thrown into sharp relief when one contrasts Melville with John Donne. "No man," wrote the latter in the

1630s, "is an iland, intire of itselfe; every man is a peece of the Continent, a part of the maine" (*Devotions*, 17).

36. Glenn Tinder, "Human Estrangement and the Failure of the Political Imagination," *Review of Politics* 21 (October 1959):624–25.

37. Cf. Thielicke: "I cannot regain the world unless I regain my *self*. And I cannot regain my self unless I regain God. . . . A program of restoration by means of a new philosophical interpretation of the world or by means of an active organizational reconstruction of the world could only mean that we should be trying to put the cart before the horse" (*Nihilism*, p. 103).

38. Bruce Wilshire, *Romanticism and Evolution* (New York: G. P. Putnam's Sons, Capricorn Books, 1968), p. 23.

39. Abraham Maslow, *Toward a Psychology of Being* (New York: D. Van Nostrand Co., 1962), p. 192.

40. Robert Jay Lifton, *Boundaries: Psychological Man in Revolution* (New York: Random House, 1969), p. 44. Cf. Novak's ironic comment that "no man *has* a self or an identity; in a society like ours he must constantly be *inventing* selves" (Michael Novak, *Encounter with Nothingness* [New York: Random House, 1970], p. 1).

41. Alvin Toffler, *Future Shock* (New York: Random House, 1970), pp. 279–80.

42. Ibid., p. 281.

43. Ibid., p. 284.

44. Erving Goffman, *The Presentation of Self in Everyday Life* (Harmondsworth, Eng.: Penguin, 1959), pp. 244–45.

45. Johann Wolfgang von Goethe, *Faust The First Part of the Tragedy*. Faust's Study Garden City, New York, trans. Walter Kaufmann (Doubleday & Co., Inc. 1961), p. 189.

46. B. F. Skinner has basically the same view of the 'self': "A self is a repertoire of behavior appropriate to a given set of contingencies. . . . The picture that emerges is not of a body with a person inside, but of a body which *is* a person" (*Beyond Freedom and Dignity* [New York: Alfred A. Knopf, 1972], p. 199). In urging the abolition of "autonomous man," he merely points to his belief that "he has been constructed from our ignorance . . . To man *qua* man we readily say good riddance" (ibid., pp. 200–201).

47. What Bellah has called "an absolutely empty self . . . a private world of great intensity and no content whatever" (Robert Bellah, "Cultural Vision and the Human Future," *Teachers College Record* 82 [1981]:502).

6 • Boredom and the School

What is the task of all higher education?
To make a machine of man.
What are the means to this end?
The student must learn to be bored.

Friedrich Nietzsche

Hyperboredom, it has thus far been argued, has developed into a major cultural force as a result of the dialectical bringing into question of the objective reference both of culture and of the self. This in turn has arisen out of the passage from the Common Human Pattern to modern Western society, in two distinguishable phases. In the CHP, 'self' lies within the womb of culture, of Being, of selfdom: individuation is very largely physical, and there is a low threshold of personal choice and a narrow horizon of awareness, with the distinctions among man, his social world, and the world of nature and supernature blurred and shifting. With Western man in the cultures of the eastern Mediterranean and above all Greece, the self moved from selfdom, the absorption *of* self, to selfhood, the absorption *with* self. Self was, as it were, born out of the womb of culture, but still remained so subject to the pressure of existence as to be only very gradually aware that it could now stand alone, save, of course, for those geniuses whose brilliance lay precisely in their ability to lift themselves to some extent out of their own time. As the self gradually separated itself from culture there began that reciprocal process which has culminated in the bringing into question that has undermined the objective basis for any culture, a skepticism that has itself undercut the objective credibility of any self. With the dissolution of the two generating centers of meaning, hyperboredom has developed and proliferated.

One question that now has to be faced is whether it is possible for culture—any culture—to recover its roots in the individual, and with them an acceptance, whether conscious or unconscious, of the limitations on choice of action and of belief that any such acceptance necessarily entails. Another uncertainty is whether people can somehow recover a sense of the substantiality and reality of a personal self, one with significant autonomy, but also with *objective* limitation. Yet a third is whether it is any longer possible for education to reassume its central role of passing on some true and acceptable view of the world, and of assisting in the development of personal selves in harmony with that true view. It has to be recognized, as against these possibilities, that we may have long since passed the point of no return; that, as C. S. Lewis suggested thirty years ago, "perhaps, in the nature of things, analytical understanding must always be a basilisk which kills what it sees and only sees by killing."[1] If so, a period of social upheaval, even catastrophe, may have to ensue before the realization is recovered that some range of social institutions and ethical norms *is* objective, although not verifiable in the way of empirical propositions, and that without them society is just not capable of sustaining itself. Men in the future might come to accept, as demonstrably foolish to flout, institutions and norms that earlier societies lived with and by just because they were there, and then reason and truth might come together at last. It is open to considerable doubt whether the realization will become general enough to make action possible, whether even if it is grasped it will be enough to persuade those who perceive it to accept its consequences, and whether it will be sufficiently clear just *what* institutions and norms are in fact essential. Can man really be his own imperative? Is fear enough to produce wisdom and self-abnegation? To a great extent the answer to these questions depends upon the character and perceptions of the selves that the process of education—formal and informal— help to develop, which in turn must rest upon a realistic view of the self and its workings, and of how education affects them.

To some, the self is no more than a reflection of the culture it is born into; to others, the self is subject to another 'nothing-but' reduction, that of biology and/or the genes. These views and their variations and derivatives, together with other fatalisms such as those derived from astrology, economics, or predestination, act to unself the self (to beg the question), and educational experiences that convey or reinforce such outlooks cannot but reduce the individual sense of meaning, especially in those who lack the sophisticated intellectual and emotional resources of a Camus or a Beckett. Only a view of man as possessing a potentially autonomous center of being can protect the average person from believing that he is a pawn of one or more determining factors, whether of nature or of nurture, and by so doing avert a wholesale lapse into hyperboredom, irresponsibility, or despair.

But it is quite unnecessary to fall under the sway of any of these either/or dichotomies. Of course man is shaped by his society, as of course he is shaped by his genes, but the very fact that the influence of both of these quite distinct forces has to be taken into account in man's development suggests a degree of plasticity and tension in man that opens up the possibility for an at least partly self-determined self. Aristotle's resolution of the apparent dilemma can hardly be bettered:

> Neither by nature nor contrary to nature do the virtues [the constructive and creative capacities] arise in us; but by nature we are adapted to receive them, and are made perfect by habit. . . . Virtue [the characteristic quality of man qua man] is a state of character concerned with choice, lying in a mean relative to us.[2]

In other words, man is born with what Robert Browning called "an inmost center," a matrix of possibilities proper to the individual, and no other. But which of the possibilities can develop, and in what way, depends upon the culture in which he is raised. Whether they do in fact develop is decided by the individual through the habits that he *acquires*, but the extent of their development is ultimately set by the talents that have been given.

If, and in the degree that, a child's experience withholds the means necessary to the development of its selfhood, or actually diverts it from its center by offering him "substitute gratifications" that channel his thoughts and imagination along others' paths, filling him with alien experience and rejecting all of the indefinite number of forms in which the self might express itself, the child's contact with his center is rendered more tenuous, or perhaps even irreversibly disrupted.[3] In the latter case it seems accurate to speak of

> our secret psychic death in childhood . . . a perfect crime in which the tiny self also gradually and unwittingly takes part . . . rejected not only by them [the 'significant others'] but by himself. (He is actually without a self.) . . . So that all unknowingly he sets about to create and maintain a pseudoself.[4]

But being is not to be denied. The true nature of the growing child demands *some* development in accord with the myriad possible to it; and if, and in the degree that, a pseudoself is forced, cajoled, or manipulated into existence, the tension produced by this deformation is manifested in the resentful and aggressive activity or in the sullen indifference (often called 'laziness') that are the two faces of hyperboredom.

Seen in this light, the educative responsibility of adults consists in a kind of piety to Being, in the sense of *pietas*, the virtue so extolled by the Romans, the virtue that consists in paying the proper—that is, intuitively known, self-evident, objectively called for—respect and attention to whomever or whatever might be in question, payment due by virtue of its very Being. Impious Romans were visited, it was supposed, by condign punishment; Greeks committing hubris—failing to observe proper measure— brought upon themselves Nemesis. What Heidegger has called "forgetfulness of Being" is our latter-day form of impiety and hubris, hyperboredom being one of its debilitating, destructive consequences; violence, vandalism, and self-destruction through drugs being some of the others. Among the social consequences are the various ecological disasters that have already begun or are impending: air, water, and soil pollution; the extinction of entire species; soil erosion; world starvation; overpopulation; exhaustion of natural resources; and the nuclear sword of Damocles. These are present realities or threats because of man's impiety to nature, as hyperboredom is on the rise because of man's failure to understand and respect the real nature of the self. Both of these failures are passed on and amplified by our cultural transmitters, the media and the schools. It should, in all fairness, be admitted that a false selfhood, in the sense of a developed self that is to a greater or lesser extent alien to one's center—the "self of everyday Dasein" as Heidegger calls it—has always been a possibility in any culture at any time. What makes our situation more parlous is that the false selfhood common in our society often seems to be false to selfdom itself. People, in other words, are not just off their own personal axes, but off any truly human axis at all. Not only is the degree of alienation greater, but the number of the alienated has soared with the extension of the electronic media and the increasing perception of the irrelevance and ineffectual nature of compulsory schooling.

It is all too obvious, looking at what is usually called the traditional school—but which really only deserves to be referred to as conventional—that education, far from assisting in the essential task of discovering and working with reality, one's own and that of the world, is all too often one of the major culprits in the process of alienating man from Being. This it does both directly and indirectly. The process through which education is carried, the methods that grow out of what Paolo Freire called the "banking concept" of education, combined with the "narration sickness"[5] that he sees it as suffering from, are themselves powerful forces parting the child and student from what matters to him, and from the satisfaction of his real needs, not, of course, to be equated with his spontaneous or induced 'wants'. Constantly to be regarded as a depository for facts, as a passive receiver of information, as a mere replay system for teacher/adult, and to be confronted with the supposed world-already-existing, in which, as the current phrase has it, "you'd better believe," must have the cumulative effect of drawing or dragging young people away from the possibility of developing their existential base, their selfhood, and their selfdom. Where the home recognizes and respects these, the harm may not be severe or lasting, but where it does not and the child learns to play the 'school game', the mask of the pseudoself may become so close fitting as to be virtually irremovable. But the center, the *arete*, the self, like energy, cannot be suppressed, only redirected, and the at first transitory boredom of a child, which is a sign of some need not being met, may, if what school provides does not in some way or another by and large cater to the needs of its clients, either force them into the acute overt withdrawal of 'acting up', rebelling, or dropping out, or into the repeated covert withdrawal from the immediate scene represented by boredom. Jules Henry referred to this process as "training in disjunction," and remarked that it

> occurs at every level in American schools, and most of it occurs without conscious effort by the adult . . . lessons in subjects in which children are not interested, for example, are lessons in disjunction, for the children become detached from the subject matter, and in an effort to escape from boredom may cast about for some way of escaping from the situation.[6]

But that is just the first stage. If the training continues over a period of time, a more lasting, even irreversible, detachment may be virtually forced upon the young person out of the desire for self-protection—protection not of the external, bodily self as against the threat of a physical assault, but of the inner self felt to be threatened by boredom, a sort of psychic brutalization. One is powerfully reminded of the process described by Bruno Bettelheim in his account of life in a concentration camp. So much as to *notice* the brutalities of the SS was to call down upon oneself similar atrocities, and so prisoners forbade themselves the use of their own powers of observation and reasoning, *but,* in Bettelheim's words, "deliberate misuse of one's powers, as opposed to temporary inattention . . . leads to a withering away of [these] powers," and as he goes on to point out, turns people into "walking corpses who [have] given up all action as being utterly pointless; then feeling, because all feeling was merely painful or dangerous, or both." In the case of the prisoners, the final stage was reached when this blocking out of reality was "extended backwards to blocking out the stimulation itself."[7]

Hyperboredom represents the emotional accompaniment of that "withering away" of one's powers that, less dramatically, occurs in many classrooms and that powerfully contributes to the sense of isolation people experience in modern industrial society. It is not that this disjunctive effect, this uncoupling of the human drive train from its psychic motor, is necessarily deliberate. The realization that the customary classroom setup does tend this way has in fact prompted many of the "newer" approaches in schools. However, it is arguable that the alleged success of some of these is often a matter of success being a less apparent and thus more pernicious form of failure. "Personalized" or "individualized" instruction appears very much in the light of more efficient ways of attaining the same results and of demanding achievement of the same preset goals—the absorption of the subject matter or skills regarded as necessary by authority and, above all, *the* "desired response," obedience *to* authority. The same can be said of programmed learning and of teaching machines, and even the 'open' classroom may be a disguised form of manipulation. This last may, and the others do, form examples of what Daniel Bell wrote of as "the change in the outlook of management, parallel to that which is occurring in the culture as a whole, from authority to manipulation as a means of exercising dominion."[8]

Boredom in school, as elsewhere, is of course nothing new in itself, but its growth and its intensification derive from the sense that students—and increasingly teachers, too—have that the to some extent inevitable tedium and grind of study and learning, and the prolonged subordination to authority, are no longer really worth it; or that, while they may be unavoidable en route to the desired goals, they are little more than hurdles that have to be jumped in order to satisfy the bureaucratic and largely meaningless requirements of absurd institutions. Earlier (but for most people in or past their fifties, only one generation back) students in school had a firm sense that whatever they had to go through was somehow *intrinsically* worthwhile, even if it was dreary and distasteful. It fitted in with what people everywhere and consistently held to be true, right, and desirable, and if one found it otherwise, then the fault lay in oneself and not in the system. Schooling, up until a generation ago appears (in retrospect at least) in the light of a rite de passage, one of those always awesome and painful initiation processes that adolescents in primitive cultures have to go through in order to become adults. The rites are accepted by all as essential for the welfare and even survival of the group and are seen by the youths themselves as essential for the achievement of a highly desirable status. Their unpleasantness, though very real, is seen as almost irrelevant, a fleeting and unimportant ordeal in comparison with the benefits to be gained.

Looked at in this light, boredom, like the suffering of the puberty rite, used to leave no serious aftermath, especially since most of those likeliest to find school boring, those coming from homes with an 'inappropriate' (that is, non-school-oriented) culture and ethos,[9] were permitted by law to leave at the age of fourteen or earlier, and they did. Even though there were, among those who were fitted to stay the entire course, occasional 'accidental' fatalities arising from personal rather than socially induced misarticulation, it might be that the very rigor and unpleasantness of the whole process—of which boredom, like humiliation, helplessness, regimentation, fear, and so on, were often components—lent strength to that feeling which those who had undergone the ordeal emerged with and communicated to the impressionable young: that it *must* have been good for them precisely because it had been so grueling! The meaning and importance of the rite would be experienced very differently if it were known, or even suspected, that it was not going to lead to an assured and vital status for the youthful neophyte, and that it would not fit him for a role that already existed and would undoubtedly continue to do so in a world whose dimensions were fixed and certain.

In exactly this way, boredom has come to assume a radically altered meaning in schools whose cultural context has so greatly changed, especially since the schools are now required by law to accommodate the young until they are sixteen or seventeen, an added presence that, given their increased and still increasing perception of the pointlessness *for them* of what schools have to offer, immeasurably increases the aggregate of boredom in schools.[10] It is less easily accepted, or if extra coercion, persuasion, or manipulation is brought to bear to get the student to submit to it, the insult to the self is all the more serious. In a situation where the young have already begun to internalize the disordered forms of their society from other sources, the usual normalizing function of schools tends nowadays to increase the anomie, either by directly relaying to them the sense of disorder that derives from an unresolved pluralism, or by insisting upon adherence to ways of action and belief that the greater society itself no longer supports, except with lip service. One way or the other, they contribute to the sense that the whole notion of norms—standards arising out of an objective structure of meaning—is itself without basis. And as has been proposed above, it is precisely when such a structure is considered, or felt in the "unwitting part," to be tenuous or nonexistent that hyperboredom becomes endemic. Thus, if it is accepted that the object of formal education is to provide for the continuation of a coherent ideology and a cohesive society, then in the degree that the schools now succeed in their customary role they are in fact bound to fail. [11]

It would seem to follow, that our schools should act rather as change agents than as essentially continuators. This certainly is the view of those who, like Theodore Brameld, see education's role as the reconstruction of society. In his words, "education's responsibility is . . . to become, as Fromm and other influential neo-Freudians might well assert, physician to our maladjusted culture."[12] But it is open to considerable doubt whether a vulnerable subsystem can realistically be expected to set about reforming the very system of which it is a dependency and of which, by its very nature it is intended to be an agent of transmission.[13] Moreover, the forces of reform are sapped by exactly that normative disarray and uncertainty which they are summoned to dispel by what Brameld calls "defensible partiality," and it is strange that he does not see that he begs the whole question in asserting that "men stand today in a unique intellectual position to build a theory of cultural commitment which is in complete accord with the canons of naturalism, empiricism, and of experimental method."[14]

Even if this is true, why should it be supposed that "commitment" can derive from the "canons" he considers so generally acceptable. Doubt has earlier been cast on the efficacy of rationalism and of "philosophies of the will" in binding man to man, and man to institutions, and reconstructionism certainly seems to be another such philosophy. Departing from Brameld's optimism, it seems necessary to face a strong possibility that there is something *inherently* antagonistic to human psychic organization in postindustrial society, to face the fact that, as Daniel Bell formulated it,

> a technocratic society is not ennobling. Material goods provide only a transient satisfaction or an invidious superiority over those with less. Yet one of the deepest human impulses is to sanctify their institutions and beliefs in order to find a meaningful purpose in their lives and to deny the meaninglessness of death. A post-industrial society cannot provide a transcendent ethic—except for the few who devote themselves to the temple of science.[15]

This is as much as to say that contemporary society is anomic in a sense and degree far deeper than either Emile Durkheim or Robert Merton supposed. They saw normlessness arising because, as a matter of contingent fact, there was in a particular society no self-evidently commanding framework of values and ways of behaving, but Bell sees industrialism *of necessity* giving rise to an "antinomian attitude," which

> plunges one into a radical autism which, in the end dirempts the cords of community and the sharing with others. The lack of a rooted moral belief system is the cultural contradiction of the society, the deepest challenge to its survival.[16]

To put it another way, it can provide men with *no* "reasons which sink so deeply into the self," or rather, the reasons which sink so deeply into the self actually *disrupt* it. The problem does not, then, stem from the repression of impulses—always a massive component of culture—but from the inadequate or psychically unacceptable substitution that is offered. To rephrase, and add to, Sullivan, even if you *don't* tell people they can sublimate, they won't be able to do so if what you offer them in place of their instinctive drives is not in keeping with their needs.

It is not without interest or relevance to note that the two causes to which Durkheim attributed anomie are still operative: the decline of religion and the anarchy of economic life. The schools are, of course, precluded from even addressing the first of these, for whatever good that might do (a remark prompted by the singular lack of success the churches have had in this direction), and the continuance and growth of the second is a further reason for doubting that schools can play any serious role in social change in America or elsewhere in the West.

But just as Durkheim, though he perceived the depth of the crisis in European society to be without historical precedent, underrated—or overlooked—the long-term forces at work, so did he overrate the role of the school in resolving the crisis, seeing in it the fosterer and communicator of the new morality that he argued was already coming into being, somewhere. The error in thinking of the schools as autonomous change agents with independent powers of value creation and transmission is clearer to us today than it could have been seventy years ago, when it was less easy to perceive the fact that educational systems are clearly geared—in fact if not by intention—to maintain the interests and outlook of those who wield the economic power in society and in the world in general, and they are not in the least likely to support (or even in any serious degree to tolerate) measures that would alter their position—"reconstruction of the economic system," a replacement of "the chaotic planlessness of traditional free enterprise," "an order in which national sovereignty is always subordinate to international authority."[17] It need hardly be said that resistance by the powers-that-be is no less a feature of capitalist than of Marxist societies: Chinese schools are changing man and society in China, Korean schools in North Korea in one way, in South Korea in another, and so on, only because economic and political power has already changed hands.

The gigantic inertia and opposition of vested interest make any planned shift of direction seem in the highest degree unlikely. If these conservative forces were somehow to be thrust aside, perhaps as the result of some vast catastrophe or immediate threat of disaster, there still appears little likelihood that a conscious and deliberate redirection of society would be enough to evoke a sense of trust and submission, or would be felt to bring man back into communion with Being, for what Michael Polanyi has called "skeptical fanaticism"[18] makes any exclusively rational solution subject to rapidly corrosive and destructive criticism. Nor would a deus ex machina be likely to fare any better, although it is possible that, as societies continue to deteriorate or to succumb perhaps to economic or physical disorder, some authoritarian regime might, in Orwellian fashion, become ascendent. However, some hope does seem to lie in Polanyi's theory that there may be a "transition from physics to the process governing the growth of thought in the mind of man." Just as the forces of inanimate nature "drive forward toward stabler potentialities, human needs drive toward solutions to problems"; as the former potentialities are actualized by "catalysts or accidental releasers," the human mind constantly strives to actualize "certain hidden potentialities"; and as in quantum mechanics there is now "the conception of uncaused causes, subject only to control by a field of probabilities,"[19] there are uncaused and unforeseeable human actions that derive from an imaginative grasp and depend upon the fact, as Polanyi sees it, that "we can know more than we can tell."[20]

It is possible to see in Polanyi's hope an updated, and perhaps more scientific version of Edmund Burke's statement of belief that "the individual is foolish; the multitude, for the moment is foolish, when they act without deliberation; but the species is wise, and, when time is given to it, as a species it always acts right."[21] Given an educated multitude, Burke might very well have agreed with Polanyi, at least if the educated had also been equipped by their schooling with the virtue of deliberation—the slow, careful, social uncovering of truth, not the mere solution of problems or the mere accumulation of data.

However that may be, there can be no reasonable doubt that if any full sense of meaning and purpose is to be recovered by the population at large, the schools are going to have to do more than maintain 'discipline', impart information, and give vocational training. If they cannot deal with the needs of young people at a deeper level than this, they will merely, and inceasingly, add to the virulence of hyperboredom, to the process of tuning out and turning off. In this perspective, the so-called basics are not basic enough, for they are expressly concerned only with the meeting the needs of that aspect of the self that one might call 'instrumental', those of the student seen as future worker, consumer, voter, and so on. But what of the "needs of the soul," as Simone Weil called them, the needs of the *existential* self, the being that supports (or fails to support) the roles? What of those experiences "which are for the life of the soul, what . . . food, sleep, and warmth are for the life of the body"?[22] The experience of risk, whose "absence produces a type of boredom which paralyzes in a different way from fear, but almost as much"?[23] The experience of proper limitation, without which men "must either seek refuge in irresponsibility, puerility, and indifference—a refuge where the most they can find is boredom—or feel themselves weighed down by responsibility at all times for fear of causing harm to others"?[24]

The heavy, almost obsessive, concentration in schools on the ingestion—not necessarily digestion—of subject matter, or 'material', facts, information, data, skills, and techniques, continues to make Dewey's question of forty years ago pertinent. "What avail," he then asked "is it to win prescribed amounts of information about geography and history, to win ability to read and write, if, in the process the individual loses his own soul?"[25]

Different as the milieus from which they wrote, Dewey and Weil saw the crucial need of the self in the development of choice and decision, in the recognition of bounds and the discovery of truth, and not in what Dewey referred to disparagingly as "mere acquisition," and both would have agreed that education should in all ways possible enable young people to develop in accord with the best potentialities in their own individual natures, to come to understand more of the nature of others and of the world in which we all live, with particular emphasis on the complexity and frailty of nature in all its manifestations.

Considering how pervasive anyone familiar with schools must know it to be, it is quite remarkable how little attention is given to boredom of any sort in the vast literature, and subliterature, of education. It is perhaps just taken for granted that it will be prevalent and does not matter or, by the more optimistic, that it is a part of the school's business to get their clients used to what is so much a part of the outside world, training in reality or, by the more ignorant, that it does not exist there in any significant measure.

Philip Jackson is almost the only writer on the classroom who gives the topic any serious attention, but even he seems to be unexpectedly cautious, in the light of common experience and of the figures he himself quotes, in his comment that the "dull ache of boredom may be [*sic*] more common in our schools than occasional literary accounts would lead us to suspect."[26] He goes on to cite his own findings that, in two studies he made, "a feeling of boredom was typical in some of their classes. In Study II the proportion of students reporting boredom and other negative feelings is even higher."[27]

Though the figures he cites show the condition to be widespread, Jackson appears to regard it as inevitable, given the structure and compulsory nature of schooling. One of the rare studies of the causes of boredom in school (or anywhere else) takes a more active stance and considers it possible to "prevent boredom by showing pupils that what is being taught is valuable and useful—and by changing the structure and content if it is not."[28] It places the responsibility for change on adults, finding that the diurnal routine, the "perceived uselessness," and the competition of school, all instituted by adults, lead to a higher *"Bore Score."*[29]

A similar but more outspoken view is taken by John Holt:

> Almost all children are bored in school. Why shouldn't they be? We would be. The children in the high status and "creative" private elementary schools I taught in were bored stiff most of the day—and with good reason. Very little in school is exciting and meaningful even to an upper middle-class child; why should it be so for slum children? Why, that is, unless we begin where schools hardly ever do begin, by recognizing that the daily lives of these children are the most real and meaningful, and indeed the only real and meaningful things they know. Why not begin their education there? It can be done.[30]

The necessity of change becomes all the more evident when it is recognized, as the authors of none of the accounts do, that the supposedly rather insignificant and short-lived boredom of the classroom can easily be a direct antecedent of the chronic state described in previous chapters. If what the young are required to do in school is perceived by them as largely if not totally irrelevant and meaningless, but, since they are forced to be there, as inescapable, they must either rebel against the tedium or dissociate themselves from what is going on to the extent that they can. This dissociation or withdrawal may very well become habitual and may extend to existence in general, except in the presence of powerful and direct sensory stimulation, force, or fun.

To deal with this alienation, the schools and colleges will have to address themselves much more thoroughly to the real needs of youth in our age, but in trying to do so they are confounded from the outset. In an avalanche of 'knowledge' and an uproar of speculation, it is open to doubt whether consensus can any longer be reached on what those needs are even to the minimal degree needed to enable schools to move on from patterns that have outlived such usefulness as they have so far had. It is little if any good looking to philosophy for a resolution for, as Henry Veatch wrote a few years ago,

> nearly all contemporary philosophers, whatever their different persuasions, seem to be agreed that our categories, . . . all of those collections or repositories of the a priori which provide us with the basic forms we impose upon the world . . . are in no wise fixed and unchanging.[31]

And the other disciplines are no less divided in their views of man and the world. As for religion, its claims have been so heavily eroded by internal division and external assault that none can command more than limited and diminishing assent.

The historical record makes it clear enough that hyperboredom is no mere surface phenomenon but a response to an ontological thirst, to the "ontological need which lies at the very heart of our lives,"[32] and so education that aims only at the epistemological or axiological level is of necessity inadequate. Head alone will serve no better than heart; what is necessary is the nurturing of the specifically human faculty for which—significantly?—no exact word exists in English. The Greeks called it *thymos,* a word combining the notion of soul, spirit, mind, and breath; the Chinese used a word which translates as "chest," a natural sagacity in which intellect and emotion were not separable; Paul Tillich speaks of it as *Mut,* usually but misleadingly translated as "courage," and he defines it as the "unreflective striving to what is noble . . . the affirmation of one's essential nature, one's inner aim or entelechy."[33] For Heidegger it is the authentic existence of *Dasein,* in which "the self has been taken hold of in its own way," as distinct from "the self of everyday *Dasein*" that he refers to as the "They-self."[34] The latter, because it is sundered from what it by rights is, becomes subject either to profound anxiety or to profound boredom.

But if one accepts this view of the self, and if the self *is* to be grasped in its reality, education must be one long campaign against the forces of illusion and irreality, forces that seek, especially in our society for one reason or another, to overwhelm it or to subvert and suborn it. And the prospects of success do not look encouraging, not least because of the ubiquity and subtlety of the influences dedicated to diverting man from his true central concerns, and the fact that they operate on the individual from his earliest days. Against these forces the schools might act—but by and large do not—as some sort of counterpoise, to provide what Dewey described as "that inward protection against sensation, excitement, credulity, and conventionally stereotyped opinion which is found in the trained mind." "Current schooling," as he went on to remark, writing in the 1930s,

> not only does little to make discriminating intelligence a safeguard against surrender to the invasion of a bunk—but it does much to favor susceptibility to a welcoming reception of it . . . by

a systematic, almost deliberate, avoidance of the spirit of criticism.[35]

The situation has in many ways worsened since Dewey wrote, not least because colleges have been, and remain, little more concerned to encourage in their students "the spirit of criticism" than they in turn are when they go back to the schools as teachers or go out into society in general and become parents.

But even in the unlikely event that they underwent a change of heart (and mind), a crucial doubt would remain: Can "discriminating intelligence" in itself provide people en masse with the degree or type of assurance of meaning that history and anthropology strongly suggest they need in order to be able to function in, and to maintain, any society or culture whatever? Dewey writes of man as endowed with "native need" that has "immediate certainty and efficiency," and he points to it as the business of "educational procedures to secure *normal* integration of meaning in organic action"[36] (emphasis added). But it is not at all evident where the authority comes from on what constitutes "normal" integration, or what establishes the 'rectitude' of an action, especially in light of the fact that he elsewhere declares that "nature has no preference for good things over bad things." If "the human situation falls entirely within nature,"[37] the basis for decisions about 'good' and 'bad' is not readily evident. It may, of course, quite well be argued that nature can just as legitimately serve as a source of value as some external, supernatural authority or revelation, but it is at least possible to wonder whether Dewey is not one of those whom Romano Guardini perceived as "deny[ing] Christian doctrine, and a Christian order of life even as [they] usurp its human and cultural effects."[38] Coming from the opposite pole, Dearden has suggested that Dewey

> is just taking morality for granted and assuming that it, like everything else of value, can be comfortably housed under his two roofing criteria of interaction and continuity. If one examines his views more closely, one finds that *morality is actually being smuggled into the interaction criterion.* [Emphasis added][39]

For Dewey, and pari passu for other naturalists, "the question whether science has intrinsic moral potentiality"[40] is answerable affirmatively. He had an unwavering confidence that reflection would bring what "morals means, growth of conduct in meaning,"[41] and that this in turn would produce choice of the good, "moral science [being] knowledge placed in a human context where it will illuminate and guide the activities of men";[42] always this implicit faith that knowledge will enlighten, and that enlightenment will produce *right and good* action. As his friend George Geiger attests, Dewey himself felt sure that man *could* develop a "devotion, so intense as to be religious, to intelligence as a force in social action,"[43] and as early as 1897 one finds Dewey himself speaking of science as the tool by means of which man could maintain the moral values of civilization, a fact conferring on it "the religious value once attaching to dogma."[44] The same faith is evident thirty years later when he wrote of intelligence applied to goods of belief as "the reasonable object of our deepest faith and loyalty, the stay and support of all reasonable hope"; again, no indication that it could result in other than good,[45] could result in the realization of part of what Bradley called the "bad self."

In the shadow of the 'rational' enormities of the last half century, and taking into account at least to some extent the doubts cast on the free operation of pure reasonableness by Freud, Adler, Jung, and other successors and modifiers, one may well be less sanguine than Dewey about the possibility of reason acting as an Archimedean fulcrum on which to lever a *misguided* world and self back to rectitude, as a neutral guide to proper action. But serious doubt must in any case be felt about the capacity of intelligence, reason, and scientific method to give rise in any but a relative few to the binding allegiance and profound commitment inherent in religious faith. Practically speaking, it seems difficult to rule out the possibility (expressed by Guardini as a fact) that "every order of being [is] sapped of strength when taken in a merely empirical way," and that "failing their reference to the Other, all things, all orders of reality, become empty shells." For such as Guardini—and they are the majority by far—

the living intuition of man the person, lying beyond and under all rationalistic thought, cannot be convinced by a secular world. His heart cannot feel that such a world pays . . . Just as the center of action is lost, its cohesion is prevented.[46]

In this situation, a spiritual vacuum seems to be created in which the world becomes perceived as void and meaningless precisely because the individual is cut off from what a naturalist regards as improperly derived moral and aesthetic directions, and in which the self becomes prey to "a new boredom of unbelief,"[47] (save that it is not 'new' except in its scope and incidence).

On the other hand, any expectation that man will succeed in lifting himself up by his own spiritual bootstraps seems, in this day of penetrating, fundamental, eager, and generalized skepticism, as has been argued earlier, likely to be disappointed.[48] In this view the theologian Tillich is at one with the psychologist Sullivan in his assertion that a "spiritual center cannot be produced *intentionally;*"[49] the theologian Charles Davis, in writing that "the certitude proper to faith comes unsought and *only* unsought,"[50] sees the situation in the same light as the poet Empson, for whom "the god approached dissolves into the air."[51] Conrad Aiken wrote of himself and his contemporaries in the 1930s as "seekers of self amid the ruins of space," who "poor grovellers between faith and doubt, the sun and north star lost, and compass out, the heart's weak engine all but stopped, the time/timeless in this chaos of our wills—must ask a theme"; but awareness of the need to ask may, in itself, render any answer impossible.[52]

Some few, such as Dewey himself, may be able to find in man and nature, in the exercise of the intelligence, and in the findings of science sufficient human and cosmic meaning to take the place of what they regard as the unwarranted cosmological beliefs and reassurances relied upon by the many.[53] Others, of the caliber and stoic outlook of an Albert Camus or a Bertrand Russell, may find enough to buoy them up, "the acceptance of despair as being in itself faith and on the boundary of the courage to be."[54] But what of the vast majority? Of those whose intellects—even if fully developed—and temperaments render them less, and indeed very little, capable of the cool, rational weighing up of, and satisfaction with, a finite existence bereft of what most would feel to be personal significance? Is all longing for some ultimate explanation of reality "immature," as Harvey Cox objected against both existentialism and theism,[55] or does the almost universal longing for such an explanation suggest an intrinsic inadequacy in reason?

Whatever the ontological status of the problem, the effects of its having become so pressing are readily observable. The hyperboredom induced in multitudes by the failure—recognized or simply sensed—of traditional meaning has already given rise to a host of more or less anxiety-ridden attempts to ground the self, and existence in general; among them recourse to every conceivable type of irrationalism, extending to astrology, witchcraft and the black arts. It seems highly probable that as these severally and together fail to provide the desired certitude, in the face of their mutual contradictions and under the assault of ever more radical skepticism, there will either be a broad generalization of the already existing panic-stricken demand for a return to the status quo—what Howard Becker called "the normative reaction to normlessness,"[56] or a mass movement toward some messianic fundamentalism, whether religious or political or both combined. In either event, the socially precarious balance-in-reality of the *thymos*, of the 'chest', will be in grave danger of destruction by an enthusiasm as spurious and self-destructive as the mindless urge that periodically stampedes the lemmings to their self-annihiliation.

Tocqueville's words of nearly a century and a half ago seem today to be more apposite than ever. "When the religion of a people is destroyed," he wrote in 1840, "doubt gets hold of the higher powers of the intellect and half paralyzes all the others"—a state of paralysis of which hyperboredom is a major component. His corollary is not cheering:

Such a condition cannot but enervate the soul, relax the springs of the will, and prepare a people for servitude. . . . As everything is at sea in the sphere of the mind, they determine at least that the mechanism of society shall be firm and fixed; as they cannot resume their ancient belief, they assume a master.[57]

NOTES

1. C. S. Lewis, *The Abolition of Man* (New York: Macmillan, 1947), p. 90.

2. Aristotle, *The Nichomachean Ethics* (Harmondsworth, Eng.: Penguin, 1969), bk. 2, chaps. 2, 6.

3. Oblomov, in Ivan Goncharov's novel, expresses this idea in terms of fire, and having despondently commented that "there has never been a flame burning in my life," he ends by saying that "for twelve years a fire has been shut up within me which *could not find an outlet;* it merely ravaged its prison and died down. Twelve years have passed . . . I did not want to wake up any more" (*Oblomov* [London: J. M. Dent & Sons, 1932], pp. 186–87, emphasis added).

4. Anonymous, "Finding the Real Self" (a letter with a foreword by K. Horney), *American Journal of Psychoanalysis*, 1949, pp. 3–7. Cf. Erich Fromm: "Early in his education, the child is taught to have feelings that are not at all 'his' . . . he loses . . . the ability to discriminate between the pseudo-feeling and spontaneous friendliness." Writing of the resulting adult, he goes on: "Modern man lives under the illusion that he knows what he wants, while he actually wants what he is *supposed* to want . . . he is keenly afraid of taking the risk and the responsibility of giving himself his own aims . . . He thinks, feels, and wills what he believes he is supposed to think, feel, and will; in this very process he loses his self. . . . He conforms to anonymous authorities, and adopts a self that is not his" (Erich

136 • *Boredom and the School*

Fromm, *Escape from Freedom* [New York: Avon Books), 1965], pp. 268–81 passim). To Fromm's comments it should be added that, since the needs of the true self cannot get through, but a generalized state of desire is experienced, people are easy marks for media promoted 'desirables', whether material or psychological (new faiths, gurus, self-help books, etc.). But consumption of these does not gratify (though it may fatten, misinform, or stupefy) since the wrong mouth, the mouth of the *pseudo*self, is being fed. In line with this, diversions and distractions work, if at all, not only fleetingly, because the real desire, or rather the desire of the real self, remains unappeased.

5. Paolo Freire, *Pedagogy of the Oppressed* (New York: Seabury Press, 1970), pp. 57–59.

6. Jules Henry, "A Cross-Cultural Outline of Education", *Current Anthropology* 1 (1960):p. 274.

7. Bruno Bettelheim, *The Informed Heart* (New York: Avon Books, 1971), pp. 152, 155.

8. Daniel Bell, *The End of Ideology* (New York: Free Press, 1960), p. 251. As Seymour Papert, the inventor of LOGO, remarks, "computer assisted instruction means making the computer teach the child. One might say the *computer is being used to program the child*. In my vision, *the child programs the computer.*" As against this possibility, Papert recognizes "the conservative bias being built into the use of computers in education as it has also been built into other new technologies." *Mindstorms: Children, Computers, and Powerful Ideas* (New York: Basic Books, Inc., 1980), pp. 5 and 36.

9. The French sociologist Pierre Bourdieu, in writing of the ideological function of the educational system, and of its connection with what he calls the "educational mortality rate," draws attention to the "blank or negative relations [between the school system and other subsystems] which are by definition the best hidden ones." What he is pointing to is the inherent mis-fit between school ways and the culture, especially the *verbal* culture, of the lower classes, which has the effect, to all appearances 'unintentional', of leading to low achievement by students from such backgrounds and to their early abandonment of the classroom—the so-called cooling-out process (*Reproduction: In Education, Society and Culture* [London: Sage Publications, 1977], p. 214).

10. One of the results of this discontent has been the revived interest, this time particularly in official circles, in "alternative education." Whatever broader and more positive reasons there may be for this, there is no doubt that much of the impetus comes from the serious problems caused in schools by increasing numbers of what are variously referred to as disruptive, alienated, disaffected, turned-off, or failing students. See, for example, the introduction to *Alternative Education Programs: A Guide for Implementation* (Trenton: New Jersey Department of Education, 1981), p. 1: "Current interest in alternative education programs stems from concerns about violence, vandalism and disruption in the schools." It is only six paragraphs later that the guide suggests the possible applicability of alternative education to the "highly motivated students, the gifted and talented students, and *even the average student when appropriate*" (emphasis added). The guide itself makes no reference to boredom.

11. Cf. Christopher Hurn: "The sheer multiplicity of diverse perspectives to which students are exposed suggests that many schools may be more effective in producing skepticism and moral confusion than any consistent set of values and ideals" (*The Limits and Possibilities of Education* [Boston: Allyn & Bacon, 1978], p. 212). The implication of higher education in this process was alluded to some years ago by the then vice president of the Danforth Foundation. In writing of the absence of any agreement on "the essential intent, the best form, or the likely consequences of students' courses of study," Warren Martin pointed to the fact that "education's dilemma is but part of a larger problem. America no longer has a unifying social philosophy, and its schools and colleges reflect that situation. After all, schools do not initiate an ethic. They transmit and inculcate the prevailing one, though they

also criticize and react to it. Today, what the institutions of education have to work with is an almost limitless pluralism, a commitment to ill-defined diversity." Warren Bryan Martin: "The Ethical Crisis in Education," *Change,* June (1974), p. 32.

12. Theodore Brameld, *Ends and Means in Education* (New York: Harper & Brothers, 1950), p. 68.

13. In a section of his previously cited work, tellingly entitled "Dependence through Independence," Bourdieu writes of how "the relative autonomy of the educational system is always the counterpart of a dependence hidden to a greater or lesser extent by the practices and ideology authorized by that autonomy . . . its relative autonomy enables it to serve external demands under the guise of independence and neutrality, i.e. to conceal the social functions it performs and so to perform them more effectively" (*Reproduction,* pp. 197, 178).

14. Brameld, loc. cit.

15. Daniel Bell, *The Coming of Post-Industrial Society* (New York: Basic Books, 1973), p. 480. Among the factors that militate against social cohesion and integration should be included rapid, frequent, and unrelenting material change and the constant need to alter behavior patterns and to adapt beliefs; the pressures of advanced industrial production and city life; and rigorous competition, individualism, and rationalization of techniques.

16. Ibid. Merton and Durkheim of course used 'anomie' is somewhat different senses. To Merton, the term generally signified, as he put it, "simple anomie," denoting "the state of confusion in a group or society which is subject to conflict between value-systems, resulting in some degree of uneasiness and a sense of separation from the group" (Robert K. Merton, *Social Theory and Social Structure* [New York: Free Press, 1968], p. 217). Durkheim was exclusively concerned with what Merton called "acute anomie," which Durkheim ascribed to economic change: "With increased prosperity, desires increase. At the very moment when traditional values have lost their authority, the richer prize offered these appetites stimulates them and makes them more exigent and impatient of control. The state of deregulation *(dérèglement)* or anomie is thus further heightened by passions being less disciplined, precisely when they need more disciplining" (Emile Durkheim, *Suicide* [Glencoe, Ill.: Free Press, 1951], p. 253).

17. Brameld, *Ends and Means in Education,* pp. 59–60.

18. One is reminded of Auden's lines:

New Machiavellis flying through the air
Express a metaphysical despair,
Murder their last voluptuous sensation,
All passion in one passionate negation.

[W. H. Auden, *Collected Shorter Poems* (London: Faber & Faber, 1950), p. 47.]

19. Michael Polanyi, *The Tacit Dimension* (Garden City, N.Y.: Doubleday & Co., 1967), pp. 59–60.

20. Ibid.

21. Edmund Burke, *Works* (London: Bohn, 1861), 5:146.

22. Simone Weil, *The Need for Roots* (New York: Harper & Row, 1971), p. 9.

23. Ibid., p. 34.

24. Ibid., p. 13.

25. John Dewey, *Experience and Education* (New York: Macmillan, 1938), p. 49.

26. Philip Jackson, *Life in Classrooms* (New York: Holt, Rinehart & Winston, 1968), p. 44.

27. Ibid., pp. 59–60. John Goodlad's latest study appeared too late to be taken into full account in this work, but it too takes boredom seriously as "a disease of epidemic proportions," and though his question, "is boredom in schools the beginning of the problems

boredom tends to generate" looks rhetorical, his frequent references to the enforced passivity of students, to their compliance and acceptance of the teacher's role and severely limited repertoire of teaching techniques, and to the constant emotional flatness of the classroom ambience leaves little doubt of his views. John I. Goodlad, *A Place Called School* (New York: McGraw-Hill, 1983), p. 242 and passim.

28. W. P. Robinson, "Boredom at School," *British Journal of Educational Psychology* 45 (1975):151.

29. Ibid., pp. 146–48 passim.

30. John Holt, *What Do I Do Monday?* (New York: E. P. Dutton, 1970), p. 68.

31. Henry B. Veatch, "Language and Ethics: 'What's Hecuba to him, or he to Hecuba?'" *Proceedings and Addresses of the American Philosophical Association* 44 (1970–71):58–59.

32. Gabriel Marcel, *Being and Having* (New York: Harper & Row, 1965), p. 232.

33. Paul Tillich, *The Courage to Be* (New Haven, Conn.: Yale University Press, 1959), p. 4.

34. Martin Heidegger, *Being and Time*, trans. J. Macquarrie and E. S. Robinson (London: SCM, 1962), p. 167. He remarks a few pages earlier, "It could be that the 'who' of everyday *Dasein* just is *not* the 'I myself'" (p. 150).

35. John Dewey, *Experience and Nature* (New York: Dover Publications, 1958), pp. 301–3.

36. Ibid., p. 112. One critic of Dewey, Ernest Becker, having acknowledged him as "the path-cleaver [but] not the mighty problem-solver and synthesizer," describes Dewey's actual philosophy as being "as empty as a wish because it contains no standard. "Where," he asks, "do we start? . . . What is better—best? How do we overcome skepticism and relativism? How do we convince by compelling proof, where is the standard of excellence, even if it is only a temporary one? *Beyond Alienation* (New York: Braziller, 1967), pp. 81–83.

37. Ibid.

38. Romano Guardini, *The End of the Modern World* (Chicago: Henry Regnery Co., 1968), p. 128.

39. R. F. Dearden, *The Philosophy of Primary Education* (London: Routledge & Kegan Paul, 1968), p. 44. Allen Wheelis makes the rather facile comment that, after the earlier belief that the social sciences would "catch up," "we now remember Dewey as a well-meaning uncle from our childhood, a guide to a more innocent world" (*The Moralist* [New York: Basic Books, 19173], p. 126). While this is gratuitously patronizing, it does not seem unfair to regard Dewey as something of an innocent when one reads his works in the wake of man's appalling inhumanity to man in the last, say, sixty years, those precisely which have seen the most immense burgeoning of man's knowledge and rational control of nature. One may, rather, find oneself agreeing with Becker's more probing criticism of Enlightenment rationalism as a whole, of which in crucial respects Dewey is a descendant, for its "easy hope that by the spread of reason men will stand up to their full size and renounce irrationalism," and with his subsequent contention that "the weakness" of the Enlightenment was that it did not understand human nature—and it apparently still does not" (Ernest Becker, *Escape from Evil* [New York: Free Press, 1975], pp. 160–62).

40. John Dewey, *Freedom and Culture* (New York: G. P. Putnam's Sons, Capricorn Books, 1963), p. 153.

41. John Dewey, *Human Nature and Conduct* (New York: Henry Holt, 1922), p. 280.

42. Ibid., p. 296.

43. George R. Geiger, *John Dewey in Perspective* (New York: Oxford University Press, 1958), p. 222. Another Geiger, Theodor, exemplifies those to whom reason is the answer. "Life," he wrote, "in a modern society can in the long run only be mastered by a highly intellectual type of person." Without apparently realizing the fatal weakness it reveals, he

goes on to remark that "the only ones who will claim that today's average citizens are equal to these tasks are those who consider it democratic to flatter the masses." He seems to imply that the masses *could* become "equal to these tasks," presumably through education (*On Social Order and Mass Society,* trans. Robert E. Peck [Chicago: University of Chicago Press, 1969], pp. 188–91).

42. John Dewey, "The Problems of Knowledge, in *The Influence of Darwin on Philosophy* (New York: Henry Holt, 1910), p. 298.

45. Dewey, *Experience and Nature,* p. 437. It is perhaps not without significance that some decrease in certainty about the efficacy of scientific method in human affairs appears in a work of his later years, where he remarks that "*if* it [science] is incapable of developing moral techniques . . . the split in modern culture goes so deep that not only democracy but all civilized values are doomed." But 'incapable' may, of course, merely mean 'in practice just not actually living up to its intrinsic capacity' (*Freedom and Culture,* p. 154).

46. Guardini, *End of the Modern World,* p. 128.

47. Julian Jaynes, *The Origin of Consciousness in the Breakdown of the Bicameral Mind* (Boston: Houghton Mifflin, 1976), p. 440.

48. E. M. Cioran, the supreme and subtle Rumanian skeptic, returns again and again to this theme: "A civilization begins by myth and ends in doubt; a theoretical doubt which, once it turns against itself, becomes quite practical . . . For the various beliefs it had engendered and which now break adrift, it substitutes a system of uncertainties, it *organizes* its metaphysical shipwreck. . . . As long as we follow the mind's spontaneous movement [what Jaynes would call the stage of the Bicameral Mind], as long as, by reflection, we put ourselves *on the level of life itself,* we cannot think that we are thinking; once we do so, our ideas oppose each other, neutralize each other within an empty consciousness. This state of sterility . . . is precisely where doubt leads us, a state which in many ways is related to the *accidie* of the mystics. . . . we are cast into the uncertain, devoured by the insipid. Everything frays in the intellectual self-torsion, a kind of furious stupor. Doubt crashes down upon us like a calamity . . . doubt was within us, and we were foredoomed to it. No one chooses the lack of choice . . . for nothing that affects us deeply is *willed.* . . . True doubt will never be deliberate; even in its elaborated form, it is merely the speculative disguise assumed by our intolerance of Being. Hence when it seizes us and we suffer its pangs, there is nothing whose nonexistence we cannot conceive.

"We must posit a self-destructive principle of *conceptual essence* if we would understand the process by which reason manages to undermine its foundations, to devour itself" (*The Fall into Time* [Chicago: Quadrangle, 1970], pp. 76–80 passim).

As a characterization of the hyperbored, the following could scarcely be bettered: "Not one subject any longer intrigues him . . . His incuriosity attains to such a breadth that it borders on total relinquishment, a nothingness more denuded than that on which the mystics pride themselves" (ibid., 86–87).

49. Tillich, *Courage to Be,* p. 175, emphasis added.

50. Charles Davis, *The Temptations of Religion* (New York: Harper & Row, 1973), p. 24.

52. William Empson, *Collected Poems* (New York: Harcourt, Brace and Company, 1949), p. 39.

53. Conrad Aiken, *Collected Poems* (New York: Oxford University Press, 1970), p. 666.

53. That very small minority who (according to Walter Lippman) "can live within themselves in mystical communion or by the power of their understanding" after the departure of "that deep, compulsive, organic faith in an external fact which is the essence of religion" for all others (*Preface to Morals* [New York: Macmillan, 1929], pp. 32–33). Lippman's entire book is a remarkably astute and perceptive examination of the "flight of the gods" and its consequences, as he saw them half a century ago, and he was grappling with the problem

touched upon in the preceding paragraph, namely that "when creeds have to be proved to the doubting, they are already blighted" (ibid., p. 36). Given that, as he put it, "the objective moral certitudes have dissolved," it was his belief that "in the liberal philosophy there is nothing to take their place" (ibid., p. 115).

54. Tillich, *Courage to Be*, p. 175. Cf. the atheist version: "Only on the firm foundation of unyielding despair can the soul's habitation henceforth be safely built" (Bertrand Russell, "A Free Man's Worship" [New York, 1918], in Mysticism and Logic and Other Essays (New York: Longmans Green and Co., 1918], p. 46), and the humanist faith that even if the truth about the human condition for which they are searching "is gloomy, and they have to build on despair, or on the other side of despair, so be it; at least they can build and do not have to *turn bored* and indolent or violent and destructive. Nihilism does not follow logically from humanist premises" (H. J. Blackham, "The Pointlessness of It All," in *Objections to Humanism*, ed. H. J. Blackham [London: Constable, 1963], p. 107, emphasis added).

55. Harvey Cox, *The Secular City* (New York: Macmillan, 1968), p. 221.

56. As he stressed, "the results may be a very thorough and rigorous tightening—in many instances, amazingly so," having in mind, no doubt, the emergence from social chaos, actual or impending, of Italy with the rise of fascism, of the Weimar Republic with Hitler's emergence as führer, and of Russia and China with the establishment of communist regimes after war and civil war (Howard Becker, *Man in Reciprocity* [New York: Praeger Publishers, 1956], p. 187).

57. Alexis de Tocqueville, *Democracy in America* (New York: Random House, Vintage Books, 1961), p. 23.

Bibliography

Adams, Robert M. *Nil.* New York: Oxford University Press, 1966.

Aiken, Conrad. *Time in the Rock.* New York: Charles Scribner's Sons, 1936.

Alvarez, A. *The Savage God.* New York: Random House, 1972.

Aristotle. *The Nichomachean Ethics.* Translated by J. A. K. Thomson. Harmondsworth, Eng.: Penguin, 1969.

Aron, Raymond. *Main Currents in Sociological Thought.* Translated by Richard Howard and Helen Weaver. Vols. 1 and 2. Garden City, N.Y.: Doubleday & Co., Anchor Books, 1970.

———. *Progress and Disillusion.* New York: New American Library, Mentor Books, 1968.

Artzybasheff, Mikhail. *The Breaking Point.* New York: B. W. Huebsch, 1917.

Auden, W. H. *The Collected Poetry.* New York: Random House, 1945.

———. *Collected Shorter Poems.* London: Faber & Faber, 1950.

———. *The Enchaféd Plain.* New York: Random House, Vintage Books, 1967.

Babb, Lawrence. *The Elizabethan Malady: A Study of Melancholia in English Literature from 1580 to 1642.* East Lansing: Michigan State College Press, 1951.

Barrett, William. *Irrational Man.* New York: Doubleday & Co., 1962.

———. *Time of Need.* New York: Harper & Row, 1972.

Baudelaire, Charles. *Les fleurs du mal.* Paris: Ed. Garnier Frères, 1961.

Becker, Ernest. *Beyond Alienation.* New York: George Braziller, 1967.

———. *Escape from Evil.* New York: Free Press, 1975.

Becker, Howard. *Man in Reciprocity.* New York: Praeger Publishers, 1956.

Bell, Daniel. *The Coming of Post-Industrial Society.* New York: Basic Books, 1973.

———. *The End of Ideology.* New York: Free Press, 1960. Bellah, Robert. "Cultural Vision and the Human Future." *Teachers College Record* 82 (1981): 497–506.

Bellow, Saul. *Humboldt's Gift*. New York: Macmillan, 1975.

Berdyaev, Nikolai A. Translated by Natalie Duddington. *The Destiny of Man*. London: Bles, 1937.

Berger, Peter. *Invitation to Sociology*. Harmondsworth, Eng.: Penguin, 1963.

———, and Luckman, Thomas. *The Social Construction of Reality*. New York: Doubleday & Co., Anchor Books, 1967.

Bergler, Edmund. "On the Disease-Entity Boredom (Alysosis)." *Psychiatric Quarterly* 19 (1945): 38–51.

Berlin, Isaiah. *The Hedgehog and the Fox*. London: Weidenfeld & Nicholson, 1953.

Bernanos, Georges. *The Diary of a Country Priest*. Garden City, N.Y.: Dell Publishing Co., Delta Books, 1956.

———. *Oeuvres romanesques*. Paris: Gallimard, Bibliothèque de la Pléiade, 1961.

Bernstein, Haskell D. "Boredom and the Ready-Made Life." *Social Research*. 42, (1975) pp. 512–537.

Bettelheim, Bruno. *The Informed Heart*. New York: Avon Books, 1971.

Bibring, Edward. "The Mechanism of Depression." In *Affective Disorders*, edited by Phyllis Greenacre. New York: International Universities Press, 1953.

Blackham, H. J. "The Pointlessness of It all." In *Objections to Humanism*, edited by H. J. Blackham. London: Constable, 1963.

Boorstin, Daniel J. *The Americans: The Democratic Experience*. New York: Random House, 1973.

Bopp, Léon. *Psychologie des "Fleurs du mal."* Geneva: Lib. Droz, 1969.

Bouchez, Madeleine. *L'ennui*. Paris: Bordas, 1973.

Bourdieu, Pierre. *Reproduction: In education, society and culture*. Translated by Richard Nice. London: Sage Publications, 1977.

Brameld, Theodore. *Ends and Means in Education*. New York: Harper & Brothers, 1950.

Bronowski, Jacob, and Mazlish, Bruce. *The Western Intellectual Tradition*. New York: Harper & Row, 1960.

Brookes, R. H. "The Anatomy of Anomie." *Political Science*, pp. 38–49.

Burke, Edmund. *Works*. London: Bohn, 1861.

Burke, Kenneth. *Permanence and Change: An Anatomy of Purpose*. Los Altos, Calif.: Hermes Publications, 1954.

Burton, Robert. *The Anatomy of Melancholy*. London: J. M. Dent & Sons, 1932.

Burtt, E. A. *The Metaphysical Foundations of Modern Physical Science.* London: Routledge & Kegan Paul, 1932.

Byron, George Gordon, Lord. *The Works of Lord Byron.* Edited by E. H. Coleridge. New York: Octagon Books, 1966.

Callahan, Daniel. "Search for an Ethic." *Center Magazine,* July/August 1972, pp. 4–12.

Campbell, Joseph. *The Masks of God: Creative Mythology.* New York: Viking Press, 1968.

Camus, Albert. *The Rebel.* Translated by Anthony Bower. New York: Random House, Vintage Books, 1956.

———. *The Stranger.* Translated by Stuart Gilbert. New York: Random House, Vintage Books, 1946.

Carroll, John S. *Prisoners of Hope.* London: Hodder & Stoughton, 1906.

Chaucer, Geoffrey. *The Works of Geoffrey Chaucer.* Edited by F. N. Robinson. Boston: Houghton Mifflin, 1957.

Chekhov, Anton. *Six Plays.* Edited by Robert W. Corrigan. New York: Holt, Rinehart & Winston, 1962.

Chiaromonte, Nicola. *The Worm of Consciousness and Other Essays.* New York: Harcourt Brace Jovanovich, n.d.

Cioran, E. M. *The Fall into Time.* Chicago: Quadrangle, 1970.

———. *The Temptation to Exist.* Chicago: Quadrangle, 1973.

Clive, Geoffrey. "A Phenomenology of Boredom." *Journal of Existentialism* 5 (1965): 359–370.

Coffin, Charles Monroe. *John Donne and the New Philosophy.* New York: Humanities Press, 1958.

Copleston, Frederick. *A History of Philosophy.* Vol. 3, part 3. Garden City, N.Y.: Doubleday & Co., Image Books, 1963.

Cox, Harvey. *The Secular City.* New York: Macmillan, 1968.

Davis, Charles. *The Temptations of Religion.* New York: Harper & Row, 1973.

Dearden, R. F. *The Philosophy of Primary Education.* London: Routledge & Kegan Paul, 1968.

Deffand, Marquise du [Marie de Vichy-Chamrond]. *Lettres de la marquise du Deffant à Horace Walpole.* Paris: Lib. de Firmin Didot Frères, Fils & Cie, 1864.

Descartes, René. *Discourse on Method.* Translated by Laurence J. Lafleur. New York: Bobbs-Merrill, 1950.

Dewey, John. *Characters and Events.* New York: Octagon Books, 1970.

———. *Experience and Education.* New York: Macmillan, 1938.

———. *Experience and Nature.* New York: Dover Publications, 1958.

————. *Freedom and Culture.* New York: G. P. Putnam's Sons, Capricorn Books, 1963.

————. *Human Nature and Conduct.* New York: Henry Holt, 1922.

————. "The Problems of Knowledge." In *The Influence of Darwin on Philosophy.* New York: Henry Holt, 1910.

Dickens, Charles. *Bleak House.* New York: W. W. Norton & Co., 1977.

Dostoevsky, Fyodor. *The Possessed.* New York: New American Library, 1962.

————. *The Short Novels.* Translated by Constance Garnett. New York: Dial Press, 1945.

Dumont, Louis. *From Mandeville to Marx.* Chicago: University of Chicago Press, 1977.

Durkheim, Emile. *The Elementary Forms of the Religious Life.* Translated by Joseph Ward Swain. London: George Allen & Unwin, 1964.

————. *Suicide.* Glencoe, Ill.: Free Press, 1951.

Earle, William. "The Future of Civilization." *Philosophy Forum* 13 (1973): 209–23.

Edman, Irwin. *The Contemporary and His Soul.* New York: Cape & Smith, 1931.

Eliade, Mircea. *The Sacred and the Profane.* New York: Harcourt, Brace & World, 1959.

Eliot, T. S. *Collected Poems, 1909–1935.* New York: Harcourt, Brace & Co., 1936.

Empson, William. *Collected Poems.* New York: Harcourt Brace and Company, 1949

Etzioni, Amitai. "The Search for Political Meaning." *Center Magazine,* March/April 1972, pp. 2–8.

Evans-Pritchard, E. *Witchcraft, Oracles and Magic among the Azande.* Oxford: Oxford University Press, 1937.

Fairlie, Henry. *The Seven Deadly Sins Today.* Washington, D.C.: New Republic Books, 1978.

Fenichel, Otto. "Zur Psychologie der Langeweile." *Imago* 20 (1934): 270–81.

Flaubert, Gustave. *Correspondance.* Paris: Conard, 1926–33.

Forster, E. M. *A Passage to India.* New York: Harcourt, Brace & World, 1952.

Foucault, Michel. *The Order of Things.* New York: Random House, Vintage Books, 1973.

Freire, Paolo. *Pedagogy of the Oppressed.* New York: Seabury Press, 1970.

Freud, Sigmund. *Gesammelte Schriften.* Leipzig: Internationaler psycho-analytiscler verlag, 1924–34.

Fromm, Erich. *Escape from Freedom.* New York: Avon Books, 1965.

———. *The Sane Society.* Greenwich, Conn.: Fawcett Books, 1955.

Gaddis, William. *The Recognitions.* New York: Avon Books, 1974.

Garanderie, Antoine de la. *La valeur de l'ennui.* Paris: Ed. Ducerf, 1968.

Gautier, Théopile. *Mademoiselle de Maupin.* Paris: Ed. Garnier Frères, 1966.

Gaylin, Willard. *Feelings.* New York: Random House, Ballantine Books, 1980.

Geiger, George R. *John Dewey in Perspective.* New York: Oxford University Press, 1958.

Geiger, Theodor. *On Social Order and Mass Society.* Translated by Robert E. Peck. Chicago: University of Chicago Press, 1969.

Gellner, Ernest. *The Legitimation of Belief.* London: Cambridge University Press, 1974.

Gerth, Hans, and Mills, C. Wright. *Character and Social Structure.* New York: Harcourt, Brace & World, 1964.

Glicksberg, Charles I. *The Literature of Nihilism.* Lewisburg, Pa.: Bucknell University Press, 1975.

Goethe, Johann Wolfgang von. *Faust.* Translated by C. F. Macintyre Norfolk, Conn.: New Directions Publishing Corp., 1949.

———. *Faust.* Translated by Louis MacNeice. New York: Oxford University Press, 1960.

Goodlad, John I. *A Place Called School.* New York: McGraw-Hill, 1983.

Goffman, Erving. *The Presentation of the Self in Everyday Life.* Harmondsworth, Eng.: Penguin, 1959.

Goncharov, Ivan. *Oblomov.* London: J. M. Dent & Sons, 1932.

Gray, Thomas. *The Correspondence of Thomas Gray.* Edited by Paget, Toynbee, and Leonard Whibley. Oxford: Oxford University Press, 1935.

Greenson, Ralph R. "On Boredom." *Psychoanalytic Quarterly* 21 (1952): 290–302.

Grierson, H. J. C., ed. *The Poems of John Donne.* Oxford: Oxford University Press, 1912.

Guardini, Romano. *The End of the Modern World.* Chicago: Henry Regnery Co., 1968.

Hampshire, Stuart. *Thought and Action.* New York: Viking Press, 1959.

Hayman, Ronald. *Samuel Beckett.* New York: Frederick Ungar Publishing Co., 1973.

Hegel, G. W. F. *Phenomenology of Mind.* Translated by J. B. Baillie. New York: Harper & Row, 1969.

Heidegger, Martin. *Being and Time.* Translated by J. Macquarrie and E. S. Robinson. London: SCM, 1962.

———. *An Introduction to Metaphysics.* Translated by R. Manheim. Garden City, N.Y.: Doubleday & Co., Anchor Books, 1961.

———. "What Is Metaphysics?" Translated by R. F. C. Hull and Alan Crick. In *Existence and Being,* edited by W. Brock. Chicago: Henry Regnery Co., 1949.

Heller, Erich. *The Disinherited Mind.* Cleveland: World Publishing Co., 1959.

Henry, Jules. *Culture against Man.* New York: Random House, Vintage Books, 1965.

———. "A Cross-Cultural Outline of Education." *Current Anthropology* 1 (1960): 267–305.

Hesse, Hermann. *Steppenwolf.* Translated by Basil Creighton. New York: Holt, Rinehart & Winston, 1963.

Holt, John. *What Do I Do Monday?* New York: E. P. Dutton, 1970.

Hoog, Armand. "Who Invented the *Mal de Siècle?*" *Yale French Studies* 13 (1954), pp. 42–51.

Horney, Karen. Foreword to anonymous letters "Finding the Real Self." *American Journal of Psychoanalysis* (1949), 9:3.

Howe, Irving. "Notes on Mass Culture." In *Mass Culture,* edited by M. Rosenberg. New York: Free Press, 1957.

Hughes, Robert. "The World of Steinberg." *Time,* 17 April 1978, pp. 92–96.

Huizinga, Johan. *Homo Ludens.* Boston: Beacon Press, 1955.

Hurn, Christopher. *The Limits and Possibilities of Education.* Boston: Allyn & Bacon, 1978.

Huxley, Aldous. "Accidie." In *On the Margin.* London: Chatto & Windus, 1923.

Jackson, Philip. *Life in Classrooms.* New York: Holt, Rinehart & Winston, 1968.

James, William. *The Essential Writings.* Edited by Bruce Wilshire. New York: Harper & Row, 1971.

Jankélévitch, Vladimir. *L'alternative.* Paris: Lib. Felix Alcan, 1938.

———. *L'aventure, l'ennui, le sérieux.* Paris: Aubier-Montaigne, 1963.

Jaspers, Karl. *Man in the Modern Age*. Translated by Eden and Cedar Paul. New York: Doubleday & Co., Anchor Books, 1957.

Jaynes, Julian. *The Origin of Consciousness in the Breakdown of the Bicameral Mind*. Boston: Houghton Mifflin, 1976.

Jonas, Hans. *The Gnostic Religion*. Boston: Beacon Press, 1963.

Kafka, Franz. *The Complete Stories*. Edited by Nahum N. Glatzer. New York: Schocken Books, 1971.

———. *Diaries, 1914–1923*. Edited by Max Brod. New York: Schocken Books, 1949

Kahler, Erich. *The Disintegration of Form in the Arts*. New York: George Braziller, 1967.

———. *The Tower and the Abyss*. New York: Viking Press, 1967.

Kaufmann, Walter. *Discovering the Mind*. New York; McGraw-Hill Book Co., 1980.

———. *Existentialism from Dostoevsky to Sartre*. New York: World Publishing Co., Meridian Books, 1956.

Kierkegaard, Sören. *Concluding Unscientific Postscript*. Translated by David F. Swenson, Lillian Marvin Swenson, and Walter Lowrie. Princeton, N.J.: Princeton University Press, 1968.

———. *Either/Or*. Translated by David F. Swenson, Lillian Marvin Swenson, and Walter Lowrie. Princeton, N.J.: Princeton University Press, 1944.

———. *The Sickness unto Death*. Translated by Walter Lowrie. Garden City, N.Y.: Doubleday & Co., 1955.

Klerks, W. *Madame du Deffand-Essai sur l'ennui*. Leiden: Universitaire Pers, 1961.

Klibansky, Raymond; Panofsky, Erwin; and Saxl, Fritz. *Saturn and Melancholy: Studies in the History of Natural Philosophy, Religion and Art*. London: Nelson, 1964.

Knowles, David. *The Evolution of Medieval Thought*. New York: Random House, Vintage Books, 1962.

Kuhn, Reinhard. *The Demon of Noontide: Ennui in Western Literature*. Princeton, N.J.: Princeton University Press, 1976.

Kuhn, Thomas. *The Structure of Scientific Revolutions*. Chicago: University of Chicago Press, 1970.

Ladner, Gerhart B. "Homo Viator: Medieval Ideas on Alienation and Order: *Speculum* 42 (1967): 233–259

Laing, R. D. *The Politics of Experience*. New York: Random House, Ballantine Books, 1967.

Leckart, Bruce, with L. G. Weinberger. *Up from Boredom, Down from Fear*. New York: G. P. Putnam's Sons, Richard Marek Publishers, 1980.

Leites, Nathan. "Trends in Affectlessness." *American Imago* 4 (1947): 89–112.

Le Savoureux, Henri. "L'ennui normal et l'ennui morbide." *Journal de Psychologie normal et pathologique,* 1914, pp. 131–148.

Lévi-Strauss, Claude. *The Savage Mind.* Chicago: University of Chicago Press, 1966.

Lewis, C. S. *The Abolition of Man.* New York: Macmillan, 1947.

Lewis, W. S., and Smith, W. H., eds. *Horace Walpole's Correspondence with Madame du Deffand and Wiart.* New Haven, Conn.: Yale University Press, 1939.

Lifton, Robert Jay. *Boundaries: Psychological Man in Revolution.* New York: Random House, 1969

Linton, Ralph. *The Study of Man.* New York: D. Appleton–Century, 1936.

Lipmann, Walter. *Preface to Morals.* New York: Macmillan, 1929.

Macquarrie, John. *Martin Heidegger.* Richmond Va.: John Knox Press, 1968.

Mannheim, Karl. *Diagnosis of Our Time.* London: Kegan Paul, 1943.

Marcel, Gabriel. *Being and Having.* Translated by Katharine Farrer. New York: Harper & Row, 1965.

————. *Man against Mass Society.* Translated by G. S. Fraser. Chicago: Henry Regnery Co., 1962.

————. *Metaphysical Journal.* Translated by Bernard Wall. London: Rockliff, 1952.

————. *The Mystery of Being.* Translated by René Hague. Vols. 1 and 2. Chicago: Henry Regnery Co., 1950.

Marsh, P.; Rossner, E.; and Harré, Rom. *The Rules of Disorder.* London: Routledge & Kegan Paul, 1978.

Marty, Martin C. *The Modern Schism.* New York: Harper & Row, 1969.

Maslow, Abraham. *Toward a Psychology of Being.* New York: D. Van Nostrand Co., 1962.

May, Rollo. *Man's Search for Himself.* New York: Dell Publishing Co., Delta Books, 1953.

Mayo, Elton. *The Human Problems of an Industrial Civilization.* New York: Macmillan, 1933.

Melville, Herman. *Bartleby the Scrivener.* In *Five Tales.* New York: Dodd, Mead & Co., 1967.

Merton, Robert K. "Bureaucratic Structure and Personality." In *Man Alone,* edited by Eric Josephson and Mary Josephson. New York: Dell Publishing Co., 1962.

————. *Social Theory and Social Structure*. New York: Free Press, 1968.

Miller, J. Hillis, Jr. "Franz Kafka and the Metaphysics of Alienation." In *The Tragic Vision and the Chrisitian Faith*, edited by Nathan A. Scott, Jr. New York: Association Press, 1957.

Mills, C. Wright. *Power, Politics and People*. London: Oxford University Press, 1963.

Minor Poets of the Eighteenth Century. Edited by Hugh l'Anson Fausset. London: J. M. Dent & Sons, 1930.

Montaigne, Michel de. *The Complete Works*. Translated by Donald M. Frame. Stanford, Calif.: Stanford University Press, 1958.

————. *Essays*. Translated by J. M. Cohen. Baltimore: Penguin Books, 1958.

Moravia, Alberto. *The Empty Canvas*. Translated by Angus Davidson. New York: Farrar, Straus & Cudahy, 1961.

Mumford, Lewis. *The Pentagon of Power*. New York: Harcourt Brace Jovanovich, 1964.

New Jersey State Department of Education. *Alternative Education Programs: A Guide for Implementation*. Trenton: New Jersey State Department of Education, 1981.

Niebuhr, Reinhold. *Faith and History*. New York: Charles Scribner's Sons, 1949.

Nietzsche, Friedrich. *Beyond Good and Evil*. New York: Random House, Vintage Books, 1966.

————. *The Gay Science*. New York: Random House, Vintage Books, 1974.

————. *The Will to Power*. Translated by Walter Kaufmann and R. G. Hollingdale. New York: Random House, Vintage Books, 1968.

Nisbet, Robert. *History of the Idea of Progress*. New York: Basic Books, 1980.

————. "The Twilight of Authority," *The Public Interest*, Spring (1969), pp. 3–9

————. *The Twilight of Authority*. New York: Oxford University Press, 1975.

Novak, Michael. *Experience of Nothingness*. New York: Harper & Row, 1970.

O'Connor, Daniel. "The Phenomena of Boredom." *Journal of Existentialism* 7 (1967): 381–399.

O'Doherty, Brian. *Object and Idea*. New York: Simon & Schuster, 1967.

Papert, Seymour. *Mindstorms*. New York: Basic Books, Inc., 1980.

Pappenheim, F. *The Alienation of Modern Man*. New York: Monthly Review Press, 1959.

Pascal, Blaise. *Pensées.* Translated by A. J. Krailsheimer. Baltimore: Penguin Books, 1966.

Percy, Walker. *The Message in the Bottle.* New York: Farrar, Straus & Giroux, 1975.

Pieper, Josef. *Leisure: The Basis of Culture.* New York: Random House, 1963.

Polanyi, Michael. *The Tacit Dimension.* Garden City, N.Y.: Doubleday & Co., 1967.

Rieff, Philip. *The Triumph of the Therapeutic.* New York: Harper & Row, 1966.

Rilke, Rainer Maria. *Duino Elegies.* Translated by J. B. Leishman and Stephen Spender. New York: W. W. Norton & Co., 1963.

———. *Sonnets to Orpheus.* Translated by C. F. MacIntyre. Berkeley and Los Angeles: University of California Press, 1971.

Robinson, W. P. "Boredom at School." *British Journal of Educational Psychology* 45 (1975):141–152.

Rubenstein, R. L. *Morality and Eros.* New York: McGraw-Hill Book Co., 1970.

Russell, Bertrand. "A Free Man's Worship," in *Mysticism and Logic.* London: Longmans Green and Co., 1918.

Sagnes, Guy. *L'ennui dans la littérature française de 1848 à 1884.* Paris: Lib. Armand Colin, 1969.

Sainte-Beuve, Charles Augustin. *Chateaubriand et son groupe littéraire sous l'empire.* Paris: Ed. Garnier Frères, 1948.

Saltus, Edgar Evertson. *The Philosophy of Disenchantment.* Boston: Houghton Mifflin, 1885.

Sayers, Dorothy L. *The Other Six Deadly Sins.* London: Methuen & Co. Ltd., 1941.

Sartre, Jean-Paul. *The Transcendence of the Ego.* Translated by Forrest Williams and Robert Kirkpatrick. New York: Farrar, Straus & Giroux, Noonday Press, 1957.

Schacht, Richard. *Alienation.* New York: Doubleday & Co., 1971.

Schachtel, Ernest. *Metamorphosis.* New York: Basic Books, 1959.

Scheler, Max. *Man's Place in Nature.* New York: Farrar, Straus & Cudahy, 1961.

———. *Ressentiment.* New York: Free Press, 1961.

Schenk, H. G. *The Mind of the European Romantics.* New York: Frederick Ungar Publishing Co., 1966.

Schopenhauer, Arthur. *The World as Will and Idea.* Translated by R. B. Haldane and J. Kemp. London: Kegan Paul, Trench, Trübner & Co., 1906.

Scott, Michael. *Tom Cringle's Log.* London: J. M. Dent & Sons, 1915.

Sénancour, Etienne Pivert de. *Obermann: Lettres publiées par M. . . . Sénancour,* nouvelle edition. Grenoble: Arthand, 1947.

Simon, William, and Gagnon, John H. "The Anomie of Affluence." *American Journal of Sociology* 82:356–77.

Skinner, B. F. *Beyond Freedom and Dignity.* New York: Alfred A. Knopf, 1972.

Smith, Huston. *Condemned to Meaning.* New York: Harper & Row, 1965.

———. "Beyond the Western Mind Set." *Teachers College Record* 82:434–457.

Smith, Logan Pearsall. *The English Language.* London: Oxford University Press, 1966.

Sullivan, Harry Stack. "The Illusion of Personal Individuality." *Psychiatry* 13 (1950):317–32.

Tardieu, Emile. *L'ennui: Etude psychologique.* Paris: Lib. Felix Alcan, 1913.

Tate, Alan. *The Forlorn Demon.* Chicago: Henry Regnery Co., 1953.

Teilhard de Chardin, Pierre. *The Future of Man.* Translated by Norman Denny. New York: Harper & Row and London: Fontana, 1964.

Thielicke, Helmut. *Nihilism.* Translated by John W. Doberstein. New York: Schocken Books, 1969.

Tillich, Paul, *The Courage to Be.* New Haven, Conn.: Yale University Press, 1959.

Tinder, Glenn. "Human Estrangement and the Failure of the Political Imagination." *Review of Politics* 21 (October 1959):611–30.

Tocqueville, Alexis de. *Democracy in America.* Translated by George Lawrence. New York: Random House, Vintage Books, 1961.

Toffler, Alvin. *Future Shock.* New York: Random House, 1970.

Troutner, Leroy F. "The Confrontation between Experimentalism and Existentialism: From Dewey to Heidegger and Beyond." *Harvard Educational Review* 39 (Winter 1969):124–54.

Turnbull, Colin. *The Mountain People.* New York: Simon & Schuster, 1972.

Vaihinger, Hans. *The Philosophy of "As-If."* New York: Barnes & Noble, 1968.

Valéry, Paul. *L'âme et la danse.* Paris: Gallimard, 1944.

Van Den Haag, Ernest. "Of Happiness and Despair We Have No Measure." In *Mass Culture,* edited by M. Rosenberg. New York: Free Press, 1957.

Vann, Gerald. *The Water and the Fire.* London: Fontana, 1953.

Veatch, Henry B. "Language and Ethnics: 'What's Hecuba to him, or he to Hecuba?'" *Proceedings and Addresses of the American Philosophical Association* 44 (1970–71):5.

Vico, Giambattista. *The New Science of Giambattista Vico.* Translated by T. G. Bergin and M. H. Fisch. Ithaca, N.Y.: Cornell University Press, 1970.

Waddell, Helen. *The Desert Fathers.* London: Constable, 1946.

Watts, Alan. *The Wisdom of Insecurity.* New York: Random House, Vintage Books, 1951.

Weil, Simone. *The Need for Roots.* New York: Harper & Row, 1971.

Wenzel, Siegfried. *"The Sin of Sloth": Acedia in Medieval Thought and Literature.* Chapel Hill: University of North Carolina Press, 1967.

Wheelis, Allen. *The Moralist.* New York: Basic Books, 1973.

Wilshire, Bruce. *Romanticism and Evolution.* New York: G. P. Putnam's Sons, Capricorn Books, 1968.

Wilson, Colin. *The Outsiders.* New York: Dell Publishing Co., Delta Books, 1956.

Wordsworth, William. *Wordsworth and Coleridge: Lyrical Ballads, 1798.* Edited by H. Littledale. Oxford: Oxford University Press, 1911.

Yeats, William Butler. *The Collected Poems of W. B. Yeats.* New York: Macmillan, 1956.

———. *Selected Poems.* London: Macmillan, 1959.

Zijderveld, Anton C. *The Abstract Society.* New York: Doubleday & Co., Anchor Books, 1970.

Index